Editor
Eric Migliaccio

Managing Editor
Ina Massler Levin, M.A.

Illustrator
Clint McKnight

Cover Artist
Brenda DiAntonis

Creative Director
Karen J. Goldfluss, M.S. Ed.

Art Production Manager
Kevin Barnes

Art Coordinator
Renée Christine Yates

Imaging
Rosa C. See

Publisher

Mary D. Smith, M.S. Ed.

Grades 4-6

Get GET WRITING!

➡ Add Energy to Any Writing Program
➡ 28 Innovative, Easy-to-Implement Activities
➡ Includes a Variety of Assessment Options

OBJECT: Crown

SETTING: The Mall

WRITING Ideas

Author

Stephanie Kuligowski, *M.A.T.*

Teacher Created Resources, Inc.
6421 Industry Way
Westminster, CA 92683
www.teachercreated.com

ISBN: 978-1-4206-3709-0

© 2007 Teacher Created Resources, Inc.

Made in U.S.A.

Teacher Created Resources

Table of Contents

Introduction

No matter what writing program you use in your classroom, the ultimate goal is to get kids to write. Well-established rules and routines keep most of your students on task most of the time. But during the course of every school year, there will come a time when you are faced with the daunting task of inspiring a room full of highly unmotivated writers. Think about the day of the class Halloween party, the week before winter break, the period after a school assembly, the class interrupted by a fire drill, the day after students hand in a long-term writing project, the first snowfall, the first really warm day, and the entire last month of school. At those times you know it's going to take more than a five-paragraph-essay prompt to get kids writing. That's where this collection comes in handy! With 28 innovative, easy-to-implement writing activities that can be modified to fit your students' abilities, your time constraints, and your school environment, this guide is the cure for the common writer's block.

Make This Book Work for You

Even the best writing programs can use a bit of shaking up from time to time. This collection is designed not as a stand-alone writing program, but as a resource to turn to when your regular writing program needs an energy boost. Read the following prescriptions to find a cure for your class's specific writer's block symptoms.

- ✏ **Take regularly to treat boredom.** You've noticed that many of your students struggle to come up with topic ideas, their essay openings are snoozers, and their fiction is uninspired. Just like all skills, creative thinking requires practice. Read through the ideas in this book and highlight the ones that are practical and workable for your class. Schedule them into your curriculum at regular intervals (weekly, bi-weekly, monthly) to give students practice seeing the world in new ways, thinking outside the textbook, and writing with abandon.

- ✏ **Supplement Friday fun writes.** Fridays, even those without holiday parties or early dismissals, test students' attention spans. Why fight human nature? Make every Friday a fun day in writing. Implement an activity from this collection and turn your formerly unproductive Fridays into periods of creative-thinking calisthenics that stretch students' writing in new directions.

- ✏ **Prevent system overload.** You've just collected the final drafts of the persuasive essays your students have worked on for the past three weeks. The students feel relieved and proud of their accomplishments, but they aren't exactly geared up to start the next unit. (And sometimes, neither are you.) The period needn't be a waste. Use an idea from this book to take advantage of the class's celebratory mood and keep them writing.

- ✏ **Channel energy into writing.** Most teachers feel a twinge of dread at the prospect of motivating their students to stay on task before a holiday party, after a school assembly, before a long break, after a field trip, and during the entire month of May. These are the times when students are the most energetic, but the least inspired to put pencil to paper. Implement fun, active ideas from this book to channel that energy into writing and "hold down the fort" until normal routines resume.

Introduction *(cont.)*

Set Up Your Writing Class for Success

Few subjects test classroom-management skills more than writing. To take a blank page and fill it with words that originated as abstract ideas inside the mind can be downright difficult. Now, imagine what that tall order feels like to students who don't think they are any good at writing, who struggle to recall basic words and spell them correctly, who haven't been exposed to good writing outside the classroom. What about for those who are distracted by a bully or face serious problems at home? When you think about how your students feel as they face that blank page, it's easier to understand why they chatter when it's time to write and why they make paper airplanes instead of making progress on essays. That doesn't mean you have to accept poor behavior, though; it just means you have to set your writing class up for success with some simple strategies.

✏ **Stock up on supplies that will inspire writing.** Set up a Writing Center in your classroom and stock it with tools for writing. Collect a variety of papers, notepads, envelopes, manila folders, pencils, pens, highlighters, and special markers. Add some correction ink, paper clips, tape, hole punches, and staplers for students to use. Stickers, yarn, and stamps are fun extras for "publishing" finished pieces. Store dictionaries, thesauruses, and other writing tools in the same area. Keep an Idea Box nearby for students to look through for inspiration. Give students ownership of the Writing Center by making them responsible for keeping the supplies organized and in good condition. As the year progresses, ask students for input when it's time to replace or add new supplies.

In addition to the supplies in the Writing Center, each student should have his or her own Writer's Notebook to keep with them at all times. Print out fun labels and invite students to decorate the covers to make them unique. It's amazing how a few stickers can create an attachment between a student and a spiral notebook. Students can keep ideas, first drafts, journal entries, and assignments from this book in their notebooks.

✏ **Make "I don't know what to write," a forbidden phrase.** Spend the first few days of your writing class planning for writing. Explain that the best writing comes from writing about what you know. Have students make list after list of ideas from their own lives that they could write about throughout the year. Then, tell them to keep the lists in their Writer's Notebooks to reference whenever they need a topic idea. Make it clear that you never want to hear the words "I don't know what to write." Here are some lists to start with:

✐ My favorite/least favorite things   ✐ My hobbies, interests, and talents

✐ My good/bad memories   ✐ My goals for the future

Now that your students are equipped with a wide variety of ideas for topics, it might be time for you to expand your definition of what constitutes writing. The five-paragraph essay, while extremely important, is not the only way for students to improve their writing skills. Any piece of writing—a poem, a song, a play, an advertisement, a letter written in code, a newspaper article, a secret file, a poster, a diary, a radio broadcast, a brochure, a dialogue, a comic book, an e-mail— can be great practice and great fun. As you plan your writing lessons, think about using new genres of writing to teach the same basic craft lessons, grammar skills, and convention rules.

Introduction (cont.)

Set Up Your Writing Class for Success   *(cont.)*

✏ **Set high expectations and stick to them.** Writing time will be silent. Writers have a choice during writing time—to brainstorm, to pre-write, to draft, to edit, to revise, to proofread, or to publish writing . . . and that's it. Clear expectations like those are designed to help all students do their best work. Make sure you follow through with swift consequences when students make poor choices. This shows students from the start that you take writing time seriously and that you expect them to do the same.

This doesn't mean your writing classroom will always be silent. Give students a chance to get excited about writing. Brainstorm topics together, allow time for sharing ideas, put students on stage to celebrate writing successes, and use the exciting lessons from this book to build enthusiasm for writing. But, when it's time to put pencils to paper, your classroom should be a place where writers can write.

✏ **Create a culture that protects risk takers.** Writing is risky business. When students put their innermost thoughts and ideas down on paper, they are really putting themselves out there. The activities in this book encourage risky writing. Make sure you create a classroom culture where students feel safe taking those risks.

Start by putting yourself out there. Model real-life writing for your students. Write-aloud a thank-you note to a friend, ask students for input on a scrapbook page you're making, etc. This will show students that writing is challenging for you, too, and provide reassurance when they struggle.

Another way to make your class a safe zone is to teach students how to respect each other's work. Don't just tell kids to respect each other, because they don't really know how. You must make the difference between constructive criticism and cruelty explicit. Role-play scenarios together, showing how not to talk about people's work, as well as how to talk about writing. Brainstorm a list of words never to use when talking about another person's writing. Post the list and refer to it often.

Finally, praise all kinds of writing achievements every day, not just the ideal essay with no spelling errors. Get excited about a title a student comes up with, cheer for a finally finished first paragraph, share (with student permission, of course) funny character names from a short story, read aloud a unique description, "ooh" and "ahh" over the illustrations in a student-created comic book. In short, make sure every student, even those who struggle with traditional writing, feels successful in your class.

✏ **Don't forget the books!** Have you ever noticed that most good writers are also avid readers? It just makes sense that the more good writing you read, the better equipped you'll be to recognize and produce good writing yourself. This is not copying or plagiarism; it's imitation, and that's how we all learn. So, don't isolate literature in reading class. Bring picture books, novels, newspaper articles, plays, menus, travel brochures, and other examples of good writing into your writing class. If you're teaching comma rules, have students search for examples of the rules at work in novels. If you're teaching persuasive writing, have students read magazine advertisements. If you're teaching dialogue writing, have students listen to conversations from a book on tape. Authentic texts will help young writers develop a better grasp of the skills you're teaching every day in class.

Introduction *(cont.)*

Think About Assessment

Assessing writing is very different from grading a math paper. There's no answer key and no numbered answers to check wrong. It's subjective, it's time-consuming, and it can be overwhelming. Here are some ideas to make assessment more manageable.

- ☞ **Consider the steps of the writing process.** Brainstorm, pre-write, draft, edit, revise, proofread, and publish—those are the steps in the writing process, and it's unrealistic to expect every writing assignment to pass through every step. Set a goal to take just a few assignments per quarter through the entire writing process. Then, give yourself and your students permission not to publish everything. If you can let go of revising every piece, your students will spend much more time actually writing. The more they write, the better they will get at writing.

  Many of the activities in this book are designed to be writing exercises, fun activities that stretch students' skills in new directions. As such, most activities fall into the brainstorming, pre-writing, and drafting stages. Differentiation tips for each activity offer suggestions about how to extend the lessons to the publishing stage.

- ☞ **You don't have to grade everything.** Imagine a little boy learning to ride a bicycle. Every time he falters, his parents shout out the letter grade "F!" If students are graded harshly the first time they write a persuasive essay or a haiku, will they be excited about trying again? Consider holding back a score or letter grade until students have had a few chances to practice a new skill. After that third or fourth practice, assess students' learning informally through observation, editing conferences, simple checklists, and student self-assessments. Reproducibles have been included on pages 76–77 for your convenience.

- ☞ **Sharpen your focus.** Focusing on a few important skills can make assessment much less overwhelming for you and your students. Before implementing a lesson, select three to five important skills you want students to focus on. For example, you might decide to assess a narrative essay based on the quality of the lead, the use of transitions, subject-verb agreement, and end punctuation. Use the "Focus on Five Rubric" on page 78 to help you do this, and be sure to let your students know up front how you will be assessing their work. Then, as you read students' essays, ignore other errors. (You may wish to circle misspelled words, but don't make them part of the final score.) Focus only on what you decided ahead of time to assess.

  If you choose this approach, make sure your students and their parents understand that proper spelling and correct grammar are always important in your classroom. Explain that at certain times you will be looking especially closely to make sure they have mastered specific skills. As the year progresses, raise the bar on your expectations and let your assessments reflect that.

- ☞ **Use a rubric.** The best time to choose or create a rubric for grading writing is before you teach the lesson. Set your standards for the final product, gear your teaching to those standards, and share the rubric with students so they know exactly what to expect. This will add some time to your lesson preparation, but it will save you time when grading papers. Rubrics remove much of the subjectivity inherent in writing grades by setting clear expectations. They also speed up the grading process by helping you focus on a few important elements as you read. See pages 78–80 for several rubrics.

Writing Standards

The writing standards for Grades 3–5 are used in this book by permission of McREL (Copyright 2000 MCREL, Mid-continent Research for Education and Learning. Telephone: 303-337-0990. Website: *http://www.mcrel.org.*) Use the chart below to match the standards to the activities. Complete explanations of the standards and benchmarks are given on page 8.

Standards Chart

Lesson	Page	Standards
Picky, Picky! Just Pick One!	10	1A, 1H, 1F
Send Spy Kids on a Mission	19	1A, 1B, 1F, 1H, 2A
Tempt Their Taste Buds	24	1A, 1B, 1F, 1E, 1G, 2A
As Squishy as a Squid	27	2A
Send 'em on a Wild Goose Chase	29	1A, 1B, 1D, 1E, 1F, 1G, 2A
Let Fingertips Do the Walking	30	1I, 2A, 2B, 3A, 3B, 3C
Play Voice Charades	32	1B, 1D, 1E, 1F, 1J, 2A, 2B
Make a Racket!	34	1A, 1H, 2A
Set the Mood With Music	37	1A, 1B, 1H, 2A
Give the Gift of Gab	39	1A, 1B, 1C, 1D, 1F, 1G
Make Beautiful Music Together	42	1B, 1F, 1H, 2A, 2B
Surprising Symmetry	45	1A, 1F, 1J, 2A
Cut and Paste the Old-Fashioned Way	47	1A, 1B, 1H
"Be Mine, Hot Stuff," Said the Spoon to the Soup	48	1A, 1B, 1F, 1H, 2B
Old Calendars, New Ideas	49	1A, 1B, 1F, 1H, 1J
Turn Words into Works of Art	50	1A, 1B, 1C, 1H, 2A
Wanted: Creative Thinking	53	1A, 1B, 1C, 1F, 1H, 2A
Student Superheroes to the Rescue	55	1A, 1B, 1C, 1F, 1H
What's My Line?	58	1A, 1B, 1F, 1H, 1J, 2A
Storyboard an Action Sequence	59	1A, 1B, 1D, 1F, 1H, 2A
Cloud Conversations	62	1A, 1F, 1H
See Nature from a New Perspective	64	1A, 1B, 1C, 1D, 1F, 1H, 2A
Take a Simile and Metaphor Hike	66	1A, 1H, 2A
Skip, Strut, Skid! Show Off Those Vivid Verbs!	69	1A, 2A, 3B
See the Writing on the Walls…and Walkways	71	1B, 1F, 1H
Sing a Campfire Song Around the Jungle Gym	72	1A, 1B, 1E, 1F, 1H
Plan a Mountain Man's Menu	74	1A, 1B, 1C, 1E, 1F, 1G, 2A

Writing Standards (cont.)

Standard 1: Uses the general skills and strategies of the writing process

A. Prewriting: Uses prewriting strategies to plan written work (e.g., uses graphic organizers, story maps, and webs; group related ideas; takes notes; brainstorms ideas; organizes information according to type and purpose of writing)

B. Drafting and Revising: Uses strategies to draft and revise written work (e.g., elaborates on a central idea; writes with attention to audience, word choice, sentence variation; uses paragraphs to develop separate ideas; produces multiple drafts)

C. Editing and Publishing: Uses strategies to edit and publish written work (e.g., edits for grammar, punctuation, capitalization, and spelling at a developmentally appropriate level; uses reference materials; considers page format [paragraphs, margins, indentations, titles]; selects presentation format according to purpose; incorporates photos, illustrations, charts, and graphs; uses available technology to compose and publish work)

D. Evaluates own and others' writing (e.g., determines the best features of a piece of writing, determines how own writing achieves its purposes, asks for feedback, responds to classmates' writing)

E. Uses strategies (e.g., adapts focus, organization, point of view; determines knowledge and interests of audience) to write for different audiences (e.g., self, peers, teachers, adults)

F. Uses strategies (e.g., adapts focus, point of view, organization, form) to write for a variety of purposes (e.g., to inform, entertain, explain, describe, record ideas)

G. Writes expository compositions (e.g., identifies and stays on the topic; develops the topic with simple facts, details, examples, and explanations; excludes extraneous and inappropriate information; uses structures such as cause-and-effect, chronology, similarities and differences; uses several sources of information; provides a concluding statement)

H. Writes narrative accounts, such as poems and stories (e.g., establishes a context that enables the reader to imagine the event or experience; develops characters, setting, and plot; creates an organizing structure; sequences events; uses concrete sensory details; uses strategies such as dialogue, tension, and suspense; uses an identifiable voice)

I. Writes autobiographical compositions (e.g., provides a context within which the incident occurs, uses simple narrative strategies, and provides some insight into why this incident is memorable)

J. Writes expressive compositions (e.g., expresses ideas, reflections, and observations; uses an individual, authentic voice; uses narrative strategies, relevant details, and ideas that enable the reader to imagine the world of the event or experience)

Standard 2: Uses the stylistic and rhetorical aspects of writing

A. Uses descriptive language that clarifies and enhances ideas (e.g., common figures of speech, sensory details)

B. Uses paragraph form in writing (e.g., indents the first word of a paragraph, uses topic sentences, recognizes a paragraph as a group of sentences about one main idea, uses an introductory and concluding paragraph, writes several related paragraphs)

Standard 3: Uses grammatical and mechanical conventions in written compositions

A. Uses nouns in written compositions (e.g., uses plural and singular naming words, forms regular and irregular plurals of nouns, uses common and proper nouns, uses nouns as subjects)

B. Uses verbs in written compositions (e.g., uses a wide variety of action verbs, past and present verb tenses, simple tenses, forms of regular verbs, verbs that agree with the subject)

C. Uses adjectives in written compositions (e.g., indefinite, numerical, predicate adjectives)

Get Up!

MOVE THE BODY,

SPARK THE IMAGINATION.

There are some days when you know that motivating your students to write will be a losing battle. An upcoming field trip, a school assembly, or a holiday party has the kids all hyped up. Don't try to squelch that energy—channel it into writing! This chapter is filled with lessons and games that encourage movement and a change of pace—just what the doctor ordered to keep your class on track when your schedule is derailed.

Picky, Picky! Just Pick One!

In a Nutshell

Turn fiction writing into a game of chance with this fun activity that's guaranteed to inspire young writers. When students pick **story elements** from a grab bag, those difficult decisions about who, what, and where are taken out of their hands. Writing time will be spent writing rather than agonizing over *what* to write. Plus, the funny, far-fetched combinations of characters, settings, and objects stretch students' creativity as they work to combine their picks into an original plot.

Teacher Bonus: "Just Pick One!" is a one-time prep activity. Make the game, and it's ready to use whenever the mood strikes. This makes a great Friday fun-write.

Plan Ahead

✍ Gather <u>3</u> paper bags, shoeboxes, or other opaque containers.

✍ Reproduce <u>1</u> set of Story-Element Cards (pages 11–17).

✍ Reproduce <u>1</u> set of Story-Element Labels (pages 18).

✍ Staple or glue <u>1</u> Story-Element Label onto each container.

✍ Cut apart the Story-Element Cards and place them in the corresponding containers.

How to Play

Students will write a fantastical fiction story that combines two characters, one setting, and one object. Let your time constraints and class size guide your decision about how to do this. Here are three options:

1. The teacher draws two character cards, one setting card, and one object card. The whole class uses these story elements to write. This takes the least amount of time and may be a good way to play the game for the first time. Students who pick up the idea quickly can serve as models for students who are struggling with the process.

2. Divide the class into groups and have each group draw two character cards, one setting card, and one object card. Each member of the group will use those story elements to write a story. This option is still quick, but hearing the different story-element combinations chosen by each group adds an element of fun for the whole class.

3. Invite each student to draw two character cards, one setting card, and one object card. This takes longer but allows students to have an active part in the selection process.

Once the elements are chosen, give students time to write. Encourage sharing throughout the activity. Wrap up with a discussion about what worked best when combining mismatched elements.

Differentiation Tip

Reducing the number of choices simplifies the game. Start with just one character card and one setting card. Also, when students share their writing, they provide models for other students to emulate. As with many activities, practice will improve all students' skills. Don't give up on the game if students' first attempts seem lackluster.

Story-Element Cards

Characters

CHARACTER

babysitter

CHARACTER

football player

CHARACTER

pirate

CHARACTER

surfer

CHARACTER

astronaut

CHARACTER

alien

CHARACTER

cowboy

CHARACTER

talking horse

Story-Element Cards (cont.)

Characters (cont.)

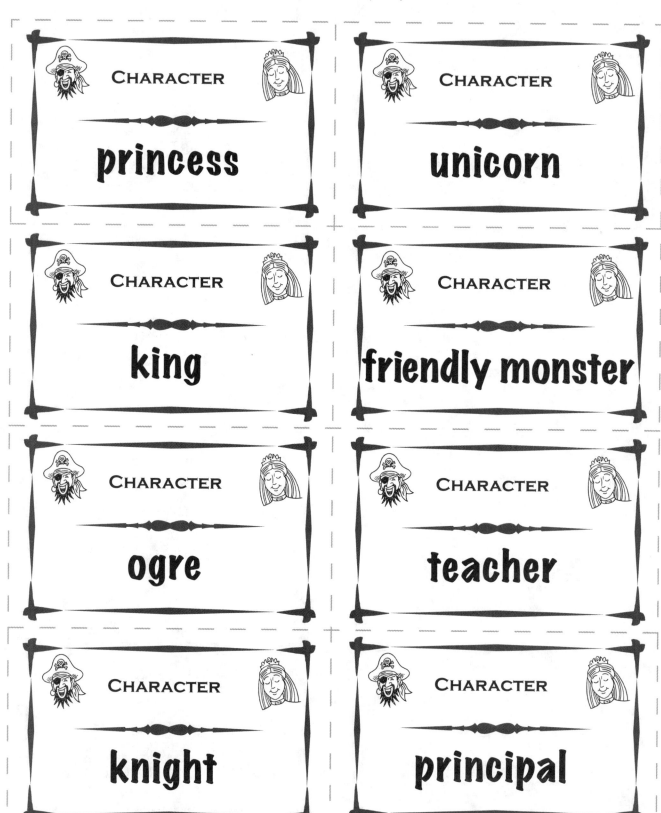

CHARACTER

princess

CHARACTER

unicorn

CHARACTER

king

CHARACTER

friendly monster

CHARACTER

ogre

CHARACTER

teacher

CHARACTER

knight

CHARACTER

principal

Story-Element Cards (cont.)

Characters (cont.)

CHARACTER
race car driver

CHARACTER
popular actor

CHARACTER
magician

CHARACTER
popular singer

CHARACTER
nurse

CHARACTER
Teacher's Choice
_____

CHARACTER
cheerleader

CHARACTER
Teacher's Choice
_____

Story-Element Cards (cont.)

Settings

SETTING

castle

SETTING

skate park

SETTING

haunted house

SETTING

public pool

SETTING

barnyard

SETTING

your school

SETTING

your backyard

SETTING

mall

Story-Element Cards (cont.)

Settings (cont.)

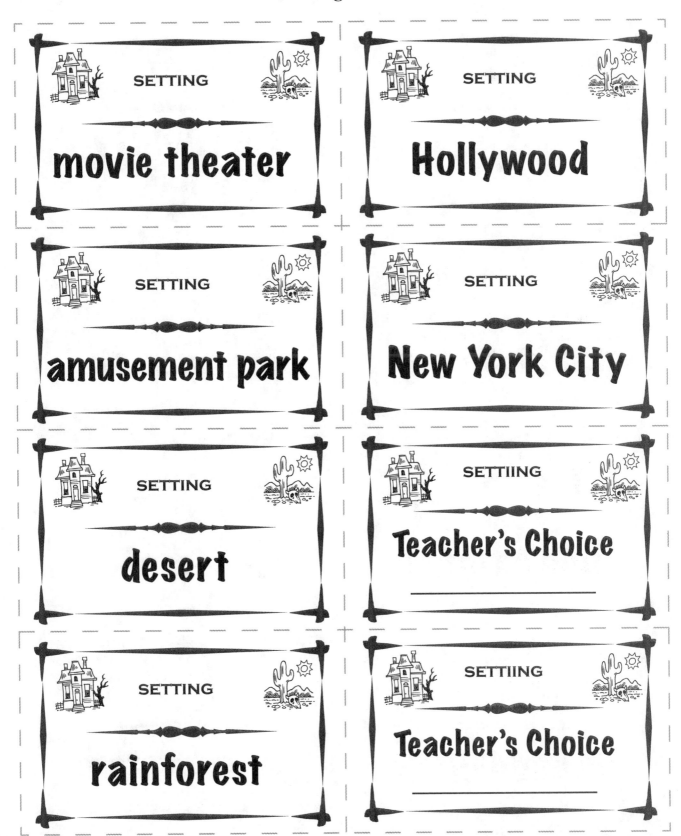

SETTING

movie theater

SETTING

Hollywood

SETTING

amusement park

SETTING

New York City

SETTING

desert

SETTIING

Teacher's Choice

SETTING

rainforest

SETTIING

Teacher's Choice

Story-Element Cards (cont.)

Objects

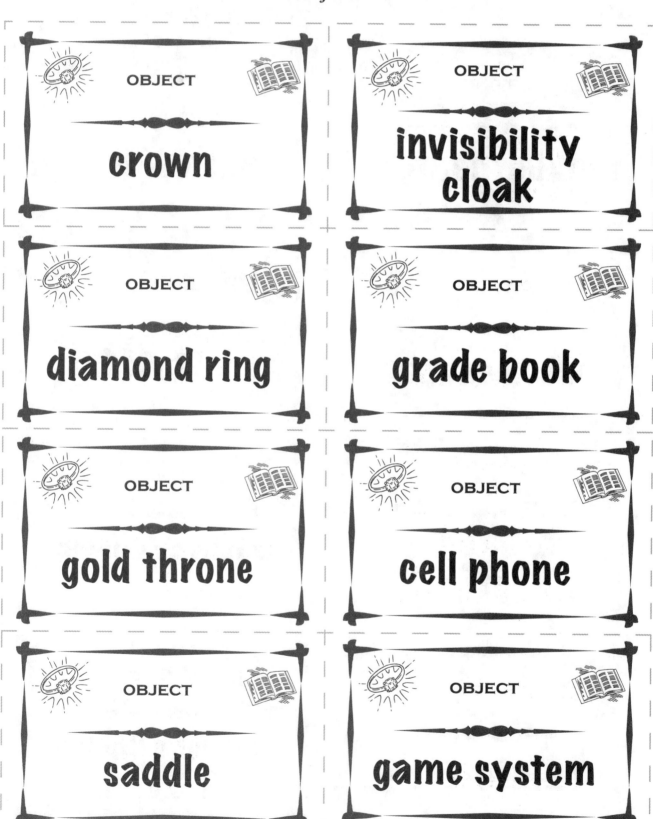

OBJECT	OBJECT
crown	**invisibility cloak**
diamond ring	**grade book**
gold throne	**cell phone**
saddle	**game system**

Story-Element Cards (cont.)

Objects (cont.)

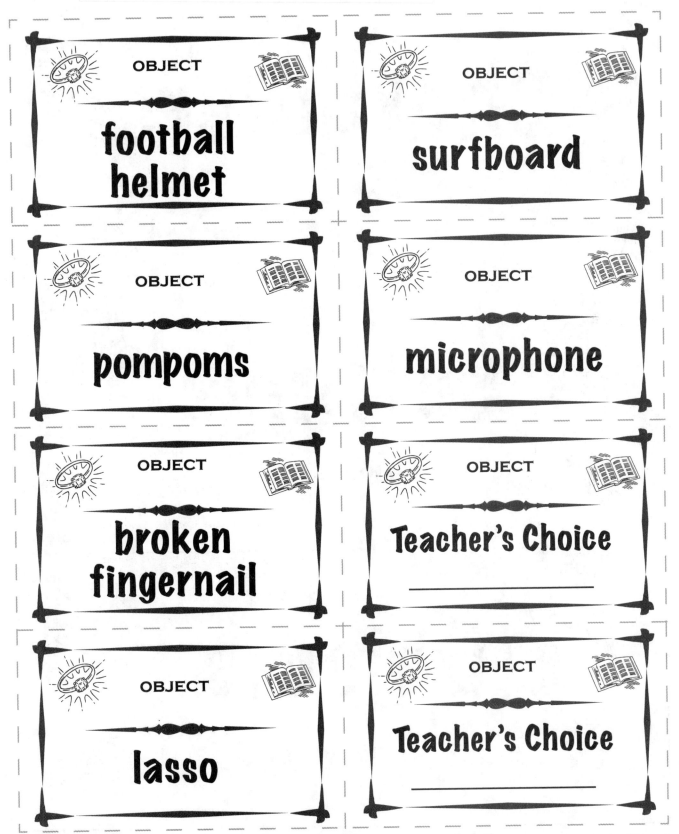

OBJECT

football helmet

OBJECT

surfboard

OBJECT

pompoms

OBJECT

microphone

OBJECT

broken fingernail

OBJECT

Teacher's Choice

_____

OBJECT

lasso

OBJECT

Teacher's Choice

_____

Story-Element Labels

Characters

(choose 2)

Settings

(choose 1)

Objects

(choose 1)

Send Spy Kids on a Mission

In a Nutshell

Kids love the idea of being spies. Take advantage of their enthusiasm by turning "spying" into a pre-writing mission. Like writers who keep notebooks to record descriptions of real-life characters, snippets of overheard conversations, and other observations of daily life, students can gather interesting **details** for their stories just by **observing and listening**. Practicing those skills becomes a lot more exciting when you call it "spying."

Plan Ahead

✍ Request permission and/or notify colleagues about the activity you have planned.

✍ Reproduce <u>1</u> class set of Mission Log worksheets (page 20) and <u>1</u> class set of Story Map worksheets (page 21).

✍ Reproduce <u>1</u> Sample Mission Log (page 22) and <u>1</u> Sample Story Map (page 23) as overhead transparencies for teacher use.

How It Works

Pick several locations where small groups of your students could "spy on" other students. This activity is especially fun when students can observe much younger children rather than their peers. They enjoy hearing the funny things little kids say and will have fewer opportunities for gossip and malicious teasing. When giving instructions, be sure to note that public places are appropriate for the activity but that places where people expect privacy are not. For example, bathrooms and school offices are off limits, but the lunchroom and the playground are perfect for gathering good information. With permission, gym classes, art classes, and science labs work well.

Spies should avoid interaction with their subjects. Their mission is to watch and listen carefully, recording descriptions and dialogue on the Mission Log worksheet (page 20). Encourage spies to watch and listen for funny or strange remarks, events, and details. Remind students that secrecy is important, so names should be left out of the log. Show an overhead transparency of the Sample Mission Log (page 22).

Set a time limit of 10–15 minutes for spying. When students return to the classroom, have them pair up and compare notes. Circulate and assist as they identify their most interesting observations. Show an overhead transparency of the Sample Story Map (page 23). Distribute the Story Map worksheets (page 21) for each student to complete.

Differentiation Tip

With quick-write activities, it is not necessary to take lessons through every step of the writing process. The goal of this lesson is for students to see how observations can inspire writing, so you can consider your mission accomplished when Story Maps are complete. If some students struggle to make the jump from the Mission Log to the Story Map, model your thought process with a "Think Aloud." Read one volunteer's observations, explain your thinking as you select the best tidbit, and begin filling out a Story Map on an overhead transparency. To extend the lesson, encourage students to write a short story based on the Story Map.

Mission Log

Property of Secret Agent _____

Code Name: _____

Unusual Events: _____

_____

_____

_____

_____

_____

Suspicious Conversations: _____

_____

_____

_____

_____

_____

Important Details: _____

_____

_____

_____

_____

_____

Story Map

Property of Secret Agent _____

Code Name: _____

Characters	**Setting**
Who will star in the story?	When and where will the story happen?
Plot	**Resolution**
What action will happen in the story?	How will the story end?

Sample Mission Log

Unusual Events:

- first grade boy in striped T-shirt chases little girl with pigtails, tries to kiss her, little girl kicks little boy, boy tells teacher

- girls kick soccer ball over the fence into the street, teacher uses whistle to stop traffic to get ball

Suspicious Conversations:

- "I can fly," one second-grade boy says to another. "You're lying," other boy answers. "I can too fly. You can ask my mom," first boy says. "What's her number? I'll call her right now," other boy says.

- "Glue tastes good," second-grade girl tells her art teacher.

Important Details:

- little boy in striped T-shirt has shoes on wrong feet; pigtail girl has on red cowboy boots; soccer ball got run over by a bus and popped with a loud bang; teacher in street jumped when she heard the pop

Sample Story Map

Characters	Setting
Who will star in the story?	**When and where will the story happen?**
• Billy, a second-grader who finds out he can fly. He spends the story trying to prove he can fly, but his powers don't work all the time. • Sam, his best friend, who thinks he's lying. • Billy's mom • Mrs. Johnson, the boys' teacher	• Mostly at Clark Kent Elementary School • Also at Billy's house
Plot	**Resolution**
What action will happen in the story?	**How will the story end?**
• Billy almost falls off jungle gym and finds out he can fly. • His classmates think he's lying. • He spends the story trying to prove he can fly, but his powers don't work all the time.	• A little girl starts to slip off the climbing wall, and Billy flies over to save her just before she hits the ground. • All Billy's classmates see him fly. • He learns that his powers only work when someone really needs help.

Tempt Their Taste Buds

In a Nutshell

Nothing gets students' attention like food. That's what makes this activity so effective and so hilarious. It does require some advance preparation on your part (see **Plan Ahead** section below). Students will sample unpopular foods and then face the daunting challenge of creating an advertising campaign to "sell" the items to other kids. This is an exercise in **five-senses description, persuasive writing,** and **creativity**.

Plan Ahead

- ✍ First, find out about any food allergies your students might have.
- ✍ Purchase a selection of the most disgusting, kid-*unfriendly* canned goods you can find (beets, black-eyed peas, lima beans, spinach, sauerkraut, etc.). Buy one can for each group.
- ✍ Disguise the foods in brown paper bags or other opaque containers.
- ✍ Gather small paper plates, plastic silverware, and a can opener.
- ✍ Reproduce 1 class set of Five-Senses Writing worksheets (page 25).
- ✍ Reproduce 1 Assignment Strips worksheet for each group (page 26).

How It Works

Divide the class into heterogeneous groups of two to four students. Tell each group that they have been asked to create an advertising campaign for a certain food. In order to write effective ads, they will, of course, need to try the foods themselves. After all, good writers write from their own experiences. Visions of cookies, candy, and chips will dance in the students' heads—and you should encourage this. Get them really hyped up.

Next, hand out the plates and silverware and give each group their food item disguised in a brown paper bag. Invite all groups to reveal their foods at the same time, and enjoy the moans and gags. Encourage all students to taste the food, but do not force the issue. Each group will record their detailed observations about the food using their five senses (see page 25). Non-tasters can use sight, smell, touch, and sound to contribute to the project.

Depending on how much time you have to devote to this activity, students can use their five-senses observations to create an advertising billboard (poster), an advertising jingle, and/or a commercial skit to act out for the class (see page 26). The real challenge is that they must use their descriptive writing and persuasive writing skills to "sell" the disgusting food to their peers.

Differentiation Tip

Heterogeneous groups allow students to help and inspire each other. You can ensure that the work is divided fairly by assigning or suggesting jobs within each group. Some job ideas for this lesson: discussion director, note-taker, artist, and ambassador (designated question-asker).

Another idea is to offer students some freedom of choice. Instead of assigning all three projects for this lesson, allow each group to choose one. That will give students the opportunity to play to their strengths.

Five-Senses Writing

Your Name: _____

Good writers use all five senses to write vivid descriptions. Practice using your five senses to gather juicy details for your group's advertising campaign.

Sight: What are the color, shape, and size of the food?

_____

_____

Sound: What sounds do you hear as you chew the food or break the food in two?

_____

_____

Smell: What does the food smell like?

_____

_____

Feel: What is the texture of the food?

_____

_____

Taste: What does the food taste like?

_____

_____

Assignment Strips

Advertising Billboard (Poster)

Work together with your group to design and create a billboard advertising your food. Remember, you want to "sell" the item, or persuade others to try it. You must include:

* the name of the food (spelled correctly)
* a slogan or catchphrase that grabs attention
* a short paragraph that persuades other kids to try the food
* a colorful illustration of the food

As you plan, think about the five-senses details you gathered. Which details will best convince others to try it? Which details would be better left out? For example, don't write, "Spinach—it's as slimy and green as a dead toad." Instead, write something like "Spinach—it's as fresh and green as a spring day."

Advertising Jingle (Song)

Work with your group to write a song advertising your food. This type of song is called a jingle. Can you think of some jingles you have heard on the radio or on TV? Remember, you want to "sell" the item, or persuade others to try it. You must include:

* the name of the food
* details that persuade others to try the food

Start by choosing a familiar tune to go with your words. Then, think about the five-senses details you gathered. Which details will best convince others to try it? Which details would be better left out? How could you fit your ideas into a catchy song?

Here is an example, sung to the tune of "Row, Row, Row Your Boat":

Beets, beets, beets are good and full of vitamins.

Tangy, savory, red, and round, beets are good for you.

Be prepared to perform your original jingle for your classmates.

Advertising Commercial (Skit)

Work with your group to write a commercial, or short skit, advertising your food. Remember, you want to "sell" the item or persuade others to try it. You must include:

* the name of the food
* details that persuade others to try the food
* every group member must have a part in the skit

Think about the five-senses details you gathered. Which details will best convince others to try it? Which details would be better left out? How could you act out your ideas to entertain and persuade other kids to try the food?

Be prepared to perform the skit for your classmates.

As Squishy as a Squid

In a Nutshell

Similes bring prose to life, but kids often forget to use them in their writing. This touchy-feely activity will make sure similes stick in your students' minds. Remember, a simile is a comparison that uses "like" or "as" (e.g., as squishy as a squid, as prickly as a cactus, as soft as a teddy bear).

Teacher Bonus: Once you've made the boxes, they'll be ready to use whenever the mood strikes. Simply fill them with different items to create a new experience. This makes a great Friday fun-write.

Plan Ahead

✍ Collect several shoeboxes. (The number of boxes depends on the number of stations you want to create.)

✍ Tape the box lids closed and cut a hand-sized hole in one side of each box.

✍ Place an object in each box that has a distinct feel to it. Here are some ideas: a damp sponge, a Koosh ball, tinsel, a deflated balloon, a pile of candy wrappers, a handful of tortilla chips, sandpaper, a stuffed animal, feathers, beads, grass clippings, a marble, a pile of rubber bands, wet clay, a wad of sticky tack.

✍ Number the boxes and set them up around the classroom as Simile Stations.

✍ Reproduce <u>1</u> Simile List worksheet (page 28) to tape next to each box.

How It Works

Divide the class into small groups to travel around to the Simile Stations. At each station, students will put their hands in the box to feel the object. (No peeking!) They will then record a simile to describe the object's texture on the sheet next to the box. The challenge is that no two similes on a sheet can be the same. Students must get more creative as the activity progresses. After the activity, reveal the objects and then display the simile sheets on a classroom bulletin board to remind students to use more similes in their writing.

Differentiation Tip

Assist students who seem to be struggling by breaking down the process of simile writing into three specific steps:

1. What is one descriptive word (adjective) that comes to mind when you feel the object?
   Example: mushy

2. What is another item or object that also fits that description?
   Example: oatmeal

3. Now put those two ideas together using "like" or "as."
   Example: as mushy as oatmeal

Simile List

Box # _____

Take turns feeling the object inside the box. (No peeking!) On one of the lines below, write a simile to describe what you feel. A simile is a comparison between two objects using the words "like" or "as." Before you write, read the other similes on the list. You must come up with a new idea. Do NOT repeat similes!

_____   _____

_____   _____

_____   _____

_____   _____

_____   _____

_____   _____

_____   _____

_____   _____

. . . as squishy as a squid . . .

Send 'em on a Wild Goose Chase!

In a Nutshell

A treasure hunt is a great way to get antsy kids out of their seats and engaged in a mission. And you can justify it to your principal because students will be practicing **expository writing** skills to write directions for their classmates to follow.

Plan Ahead

- ✍ Request permission and/or notify colleagues about the activity you have planned.

- ✍ Collect one brown paper bag or other opaque container for each group.

- ✍ Choose one secret object for each group. You could use ordinary things like a chalkboard eraser, a dictionary, and a globe. Or you could dig a little deeper into your cabinets for quirky things, like that stuffed monkey you got as a gift from a student last year.

How It Works

Divide the class into heterogeneous groups of two to four students. Give each group a bag containing a "secret" object. Tell students they will hide the object somewhere in the school for their classmates to find.

Next, lead the class on a walk around the school so they can plan out their hiding spots and directions. This is the time to set boundaries for the hiding spots. If the school office is off limits, make it clear now. Allow group members to walk together and make plans and notes for the perfect hiding spot. The secrecy of the mission should help keep hallway chatter to a whisper.

When the class returns from the tour, send one student at a time to hide an object in the agreed-upon location. (If you feel it's necessary, you could set a timer for each student to prevent aimless wandering.) Groups should spread out around the classroom and begin writing step-by-step directions leading their classmates on a wild goose chase around the school to find the secret object.

Place finished directions in a grab bag and invite groups to pick a set. Each group will then set out to find the hidden treasures. When groups return (with or without the objects), a follow-up discussion about clear, specific expository writing will make a memorable impact! Groups whose directions were unsuccessful could rewrite them, using feedback from their peers.

Differentiation Tip

Heterogeneous groups allow students to help and inspire each other. You can ensure that the work is divided fairly by assigning or suggesting jobs within each group. Some job ideas for this lesson: discussion director, note-taker (makes notes during the school tour), writer, and runner (the person who hides the object and tests the directions).

If a group seems to be struggling, set a limit to the number of steps they can include. The fewer steps, the easier it will be to write correct directions. On the other hand, if a group is ready for a challenge, encourage them to include more steps by adding twists, turns, and backtracking into the directions.

Let Fingertips Do the Walking

In a Nutshell

Sending kids to look up words in a **dictionary** or **thesaurus** is guaranteed to elicit a chorus of moans and groans. You can change that by turning the chore into a simple game. Students will use a thesaurus to encrypt a simple message in **synonyms**. The real fun comes when classmates trade papers and try to decipher each other's work. They'll soon see that a dictionary is a necessary tool for cracking their classmates' "codes."

Teacher Bonus: This game requires no advance preparation! That makes it perfect for those days when unexpected events derail your regularly scheduled lesson.

Plan Ahead

✍ Each pair of students will need 1 dictionary and 1 thesaurus.

How It Works

Divide the class into heterogeneous pairs. This activity will work best if kids already know the basics of dictionary and thesaurus use, but review these skills, if necessary. You should also remind students that synonyms are words with the same meaning.

Next, ask student pairs to work together to write one paragraph about a topic you will assign. Keep the topic simple so students won't struggle for writing ideas. Also, avoid making the topic too broad. This is one time you want your students to keep it short. Here are some topic suggestions:

* ✱ A Very Bad Morning
* ✱ The New Kid
* ✱ A Strange Recess
* ✱ The Best Present Ever
* ✱ A Crazy Bus Ride

Now, direct the pairs to encrypt their paragraphs in synonyms. They should use a thesaurus to find the most interesting and unusual replacement words to trick their classmates. The goal is to replace as many nouns, verbs, adjectives, and adverbs as possible to trick their classmates. Have students keep track of the number of words they replace. You could award prizes to the pairs who use the most synonyms.

Students will then trade encrypted paragraphs and try to decode the messages on a separate sheet of paper. Encourage students to use the thesaurus and dictionary to help them crack the codes.

Wrap up the activity by having pairs compare how closely their decoded works match the originals. Since the purpose of this activity is to get students to practice using the dictionary and thesaurus, your mission is accomplished no matter how the final products turn out. In fact, the further off the mark they are, the more students will enjoy the game!

Differentiation Tip

To simplify the game, ask students to replace only one or two parts of speech. For example, have them replace nouns and verbs, or just verbs.

Heterogeneous pairings also allow students to support each other's learning. You can ensure that the work is divided fairly by making students take turns writing and looking up words. Set a timer for 10 minutes. When the timer dings, students must switch jobs. Continue using the timer throughout the game.

Get Noisy!

SILENCE MAY BE A VIRTUE, BUT IT'S NOT GONNA HAPPEN TODAY!

When your students are rowdy, it's easy to write off that class period, that day, or that week as lost teaching time. Lose that notion of wasted time! Make noise an inspiration for writing rather than a hindrance. This chapter is filled with lessons and games that give students a chance to make a racket and then write about it. Think of these activities as the placebo that will make students think they're having fun when, really, they're learning!

Play Voice Charades

In a Nutshell

Instead of clamping down on your class clowns, put them on stage and let them shine. This twist on the game of Charades really appeals to students who crave the spotlight. It also reinforces the concept of writing with voice for the whole class.

Voice is the personality behind the written words. Adding voice helps students with everything from improving their fiction to acing standardized tests. To practice the concept of writing with voice, read aloud several examples of novels and picture books where the characters' personalities come through loud and clear. Some great authors to look to for examples are Richard Peck, Esme Raji Codell, Lemony Snicket, Sharon Creech, Dr. Seuss, Cynthia Rylant, and David Shannon.

Teacher Bonus: Voice Charades is a one-time prep activity. Make the game, and it's ready to use whenever the mood strikes. This makes a great Friday fun-write.

Plan Ahead

- ✍ Locate <u>1</u> paper bag, shoebox, or other opaque container.
- ✍ Reproduce <u>1</u> set of Charades Cards (page 33).
- ✍ Cut apart the Charades Cards and place them in the container.

How It Works

Invite brave volunteers to the front of the classroom to draw a Charades Card. Explain to the class that each Charades Card has a well-known personality type on it. Make it clear that it is not a famous person, but rather a type of person or character. Ask the volunteer to look at the card and think about how that character would greet the class. Ask the volunteer these questions in front of the class so that everyone catches on:

- ✱ *What would the person's voice show about his or her personality?*
- ✱ *Would the person be quiet and shy or loud and bubbly?*
- ✱ *Would he or she speak slowly or quickly?*
- ✱ *Would the person use any special jargon or slang that would be a clue to his or her personality?*

The student then performs the voice-filled greeting, and the class gets three chances to guess the person's identity.

You may wish to begin with a demonstration. For example, you might say, "Greetings, earthlings. I come in peace," in a flat and computerized voice. Or, in a tough drawl you could say, "Howdy, pardners. I'm the fastest draw in this 'ere town." Ask the class to guess your identity. Then, explain how you combined tone and jargon to convey personality, just as writers do when creating characters in stories.

After several rounds of Voice Charades, display the Charades Cards on the board. Ask each student to choose one of the personalities and write a one-paragraph introduction filled with voice. Give students time to share their introductions and allow the class to guess the character behind the voice.

Differentiation Tip

To extend the lesson, encourage students to build a story around their character.

Charades Cards

CHARADE **coach**	CHARADE **alien**
CHARADE **teacher**	CHARADE **cheerleader**
CHARADE **grandma/grandpa**	CHARADE **toddler**
CHARADE **cowboy/cowgirl**	CHARADE **teenager**
CHARADE **king/queen**	CHARADE **surfer**

Make a Racket!

In a Nutshell

Onomatopoeia may be fun to say, but it's even more fun to practice when you equip students with noisemakers. Onomatopoeia words are words that imitate sounds. Some examples are *splat, smack, click, boom, twang,* and *whoosh.* Engage students in a lesson they won't soon forget by having them first make noises and then describe them with onomatopoeia words.

Teacher Bonus: This is a great activity to inspire students who struggle with writing. "Playing" with sports equipment during Language Arts class can really change a student's attitude about creative writing!

Plan Ahead

✍ Collect a variety of objects that students can use to make noises. Sports equipment works great.

✍ Have a large sheet of chart paper or construction paper ready to make a class onomatopoeia word list.

✍ Reproduce <u>1</u> overhead transparency of Sample Onomatopoeia Poems (page 35).

✍ Reproduce <u>1</u> class set of Poetry that Makes a Racket worksheets (page 36).

How It Works

Move to an area where you'll have plenty of room and won't disturb anyone, like the playground, gym, or cafeteria. Ask one volunteer at a time to demonstrate the sound effects of a particular object. Have them dribble a basketball, bounce a tennis ball, serve a birdie, bump a volleyball, etc. As the volunteers make the sound effects, the rest of the class should listen carefully. Call on students to describe the sounds with onomatopoeia words. On chart paper, record student suggestions and compile a class list.

Return to the classroom to share the Sample Onomatopoeia Poems transparency (page 35). Discuss the elements of the two sample poems. Model the writing process by working with your students to write an onomatopoeia poem together. Use the blank lines on the transparency for the shared-writing activity.

Then, ask students to complete the top portion of the Poetry that Makes a Racket sheet (page 36) by writing a three- to five-line onomatopoeia poem about one of the activities demonstrated in class. The first word of each line should be an onomatopoeia word.

Next, students will complete the bottom portion of the Poetry that Makes a Racket sheet. Independently, each student will brainstorm a list of onomatopoeia words for a favorite activity. Working from the list, students will write another three- to five-line onomatopoeia poem about the activity.

Differentiation Tip

This activity is designed to take students step-by-step through the writing process from teacher-guided brainstorming to shared writing to independent practice. Some students may be able to make the jump from the sound-effects portion of the activity directly to independent writing. If they've got the hang of it, let them run with their ideas!

Sample Onomatopoeia Poems

Learning to Dive

Splish splash—I wiggle my toes in the water to see how it feels.

Slap, slap, slap—I position my feet perfectly on the pool's edge.

Ahhhhh—I suck in as much air as my lungs can hold and lean
forward with my hands above my head.

Ker-splat! My belly smacks the water first.

I guess I'll keep practicing.

My Best Buddy

Jingle, jangle, jingle, jangle—his metal tags ring like bells.

Thwap, thwap, thwap—his tail smacks the screen door.

Woof! Woof! Woof! He's barking now.

Slurrrp! He soaks my face with wet kisses.

My dog is so excited when I get home from school.

_____

_____

_____

_____

_____

Poetry that Makes a Racket

Your Name: _____

Part 1 Directions: Use the onomatopoeia words from the class list to write a poem. Begin each sentence with an onomatopoeia word. The poem should describe the subject so clearly that a reader could actually hear the action. Your poem should be about five lines long. Be creative and have fun!

_____

_____

_____

_____

_____

Part 2 Directions: Think of a hobby or activity that you enjoy. Maybe it's playing video games, spending time with your dog, swimming, or baking brownies. On the lines below, brainstorm a list of sounds (onomatopoeia words) you hear as you do that activity. Next, write an onomatopoeia poem describing that activity. Follow the same format you followed above. Begin each sentence with an onomatopoeia word. Your poem should be about five lines long.

Word List: _____ _____ _____ _____ _____

_____ _____ _____ _____ _____

_____

_____

_____

_____

_____

Set the Mood with Music

In a Nutshell

Teaching tone and mood is a challenge most fourth-, fifth-, and sixth-grade teachers are in
no mood to tackle. This activity will get the idea across loud and clear. By filling your
writing classroom with music, you will capture students' attention, expand their horizons and
introduce them to those tricky story elements.

Plan Ahead

✍ Gather a variety of music samples—everything from jazz to bluegrass to rap to rock 'n' roll.
  It's especially fun to use songs from different cultures—polka, Hawaiian ukulele music, Celtic
  ballads, German brass bands, Native American drumming, etc. Your school's music teacher
  might be a great resource, and your local library's CD section can probably provide a wide range
  of music samples.

✍ Reproduce <u>1</u> class set of Exploring Tone and Mood worksheets (page 38).

✍ Reproduce <u>1</u> overhead transparency of Exploring Tone and Mood (page 38) for teacher use.

How It Works

When you've gathered your tunes, set your class's dial to easy listening. Turn down the lights and
reduce visual distractions so students can focus on the sounds. Play one song (or part of a song).
Then, facilitate discussion about the feelings the music evoked. Ask these questions:

✱ *Was the beat fast or slow?*

✱ *Did it relax you or boost your energy?*

✱ *What emotions did the sounds of the instruments and/or vocals create?*

✱ *Did the music remind you of anything else?*

Repeat this format with three or four other music samples.

Next, make the connection to writing. Musicians use different pacing and different musical expressions
to set the tone and mood of a song—and writers do the same with words. The pace of a character's
dialogue, the length of the sentences, and the choice of words all work together to set the tone and
mood of a story.

Begin by reading passages aloud from several different genres to help students see tone and mood at
work. Hand out the Exploring Tone and Mood sheet (page 38). Brainstorm as a class the techniques a
writer uses to set the tone for specific genres, such as horror, humor, action, and mystery.

Now, challenge students to write a short story using tone and mood as a story element.

Differentiation Tip

To help struggling students, assign the tone and mood for the story they will write rather than letting
them set their own. For example, "dark and spooky" makes a great starting point.

Exploring Tone and Mood

Your Name: _____

	Describe the tone and mood that best fit this genre.	*What are some specific words an author might include in a story to show that tone and mood?*	*Would long or short sentences fit the tone and mood better?*	*Would the main events happen right away or would the plot slowly unfold?*
Horror				
Humor				
Action				
Mystery				

Give the Gift of Gab

In a Nutshell

Intermediate students who don't love to gab are more rare than the spotted owl, so make your class's chatter work for you. Turn your students into roving reporters with a **personality profile** due on deadline. This assignment is a great introduction to **journalism**, and it provides solid **expository writing** practice.

Teacher Bonus: This activity could span several class periods. That makes it the perfect remedy for weeks when you know your class will be out of its routine, such as the week of standardized testing or the weeks before winter break and after spring break.

Plan Ahead

✍ Choose a published personality profile to read to your students. Your local newspaper, kids' magazines, and the Internet are great places to find articles about people. *Hint: If students can relate to the article's subject, they will be more engaged in the activity—choose a profile about a famous athlete, celebrity, or local hero.*

✍ Have a large sheet of chart paper or construction paper ready to make a class list of questions.

✍ Reproduce 1 class set of Q&A worksheets (page 40) and 1 class set of Extra! Extra! Write All About It! worksheets, front-to-back (page 41).

How It Works

Step 1—Writing Good Questions. Start by reading aloud a personality profile. The first time, just let the students listen and enjoy. Then, reread the article aloud more slowly. Ask students to try to figure out what questions the reporter asked to gather this information from the subject. Record the responses on chart paper. Ask students to think of other questions the reporter could have asked. Add those questions to the chart paper.

Now, assign students the task of writing a personality profile of one of their classmates. Using the list on the board as inspiration, each student will write at least 10 open-ended questions on the Q&A worksheet (page 40). Steer students away from asking, "What's your favorite color?" and toward more revealing questions, such as, "What three things are most important to you?" and "How would your best friends describe you?" Remember to instruct students about any questions that are off limits in the classroom.

Step 2—The Interview. Have students arrange their seats so they are sitting face-to-face across from each other. Give them 10 minutes to interview each other. The pair must only talk about the first interviewee. When the time is up, they can then switch roles. This will push students to share more information with each other.

Step 3—The Final Product. Hand out copies of Extra! Extra! Write All About It! (page 41). Guide students through the process of choosing the most interesting facts from the interviews to build their profiles around.

Differentiation Tip

To simplify, the class could group-interview one subject, such as the school principal, a class visitor, or you. With this method, ask each student to prepare a list of three open-ended questions. After the interview, model the process of choosing the most interesting fact for the lead and then building the story around that. Together, the class could complete a profile on chart paper, or each student could write his or her own.

Q&A

Your Name: _____

Now it's your turn to ask the questions! To prepare for your interview, make a list of at least 10 questions. They should be the kind of questions that will help you get to know the person you are interviewing better. Avoid asking questions that will be answered with just a "yes" or a "no."

Subject's Name: _____

1. Q: _____

A: _____

2. Q: _____

A: _____

3. Q: _____

A: _____

4. Q: _____

A: _____

5. Q: _____

A: _____

6. Q: _____

A: _____

7. Q: _____

A: _____

8. Q: _____

A: _____

9. Q: _____

A: _____

10. Q: _____

A: _____

Extra! Extra!
Write All About It!

Your Name: _____

Now that you've gotten the scoop on your subject, it's time to turn it into a story. With so much information, it may be hard to know how to begin writing. **Here's a tip:** start with the most interesting fact and build your profile on that. Think of it as kind of a theme for your profile. Then, use only the information that fits with that theme. It's okay to leave out details that don't fit.

Most interesting fact: _____

_____

> Now, go back to your Q&A worksheet. Reread all the information you learned. Decide what fits and what does not. Number the facts in the order of what you will write first, second, third, and so on. This is a quick way to organize your ideas. When you have a plan for writing, compose your profile on the lines below.

_____

_____

_____

_____

_____

_____

_____

Make Beautiful Music Together

In a Nutshell

The writing technique of **personification** will come to life for your students when they get to make musical instruments "talk" to each other. They will really need to tap into their creative resources to write a secret conversation between a saxophone and a snare drum or a noisy argument between a tuba and a flute.

Teacher Bonus: This activity requires very little advance preparation on your part! It's also a great activity to inspire students who struggle with writing. Playing musical instruments during Language Arts class can really change a student's attitude about creative writing!

Plan Ahead

✍ You will need a few different instruments for students to play during this activity. (They just have to be able to make sounds with the instruments; Mozart and Beethoven are not necessary for this to work!) Either ask students to bring instruments from home (with parent permission of course) or ask to borrow some simple noisemakers from your school's music department.

✍ *Optional:* Reproduce <u>1</u> overhead transparency of Sample Instrument Dialogue (page 43) to show students how to punctuate conversations.

How It Works

Choose two instruments to have a "conversation." Explain to the student musicians that you want their instruments to "talk" to each other. First, one student will play a few notes. Then, the other student will play a few. Then, the other student will answer back musically, and so on.

Ask the class to think about what the instruments might have said to each other. This is a great way to introduce the writing technique of personification, which is giving human qualities to inanimate objects. Here are some questions to ask aloud to spark imaginations:

✱ *If the instruments were people, what would they look like?*

✱ *Would they be boys or girls?*

✱ *What feelings did they show—joy, anger, sadness, amusement?*

✱ *What personalities did they have? Were they outgoing or shy, funny or serious, bossy or helpful?*

✱ *What could these two characters be talking to each other about? Are they friends or enemies? Are they getting along or disagreeing?*

During the class discussion, each student could be jotting down answers in his or her writer's notebook or on scrap paper. When students seem to be on the right track, ask them to write a conversation, or dialogue, between the two instruments. Allow time for several students to read their writing aloud. That will help inspire students who are struggling with the exercise. Repeat the musical "conversations" and questioning as time allows. Students' responses should improve as the activity progresses.

Differentiation Tip

If you anticipate that some students might struggle to keep up with this activity, create a list of questions for them to answer. Having the questions in print might be helpful for some learners.

Sample Instrument Dialogue

"Good day!" chirped the flute.

"No, it's not," moaned the tuba. "I think it stinks!"

"Birds are singing, bees are buzzing, and the sun is shining brightly," trilled the flute. "Why are you so sad?"

"Why are you so happy?" boomed the tuba. "Just go away!"

Rules for Writing Dialogue:

1. Quotation marks are used in dialogue (conversations) around words that a character said out loud.

   Example: "Good day!" chirped the flute.

2. Each time a new character begins to speak, he or she gets a new paragraph.

   Example: "Good day!" chirped the flute.

   "What's so good about it?" moaned the tuba. "I think it stinks!"

3. Commas, exclamation points, periods, and question marks are placed inside quotation marks. A period or other end mark goes at the end of the whole sentence.

   Example: "No it's not," moaned the tuba. "I think it stinks!"

Get Messy!

LET THEM COLOR OUTSIDE THE LINES, AND THEY JUST MIGHT START THINKING OUTSIDE THE BOX.

"I don't know what to write!" is a cry too often heard in the 4th-, 5th-, and 6th-grade classrooms. In preschool, every child is a creative genius. But by the time many kids reach adolescence, they have censored their creative urges right out of existence. Kids need inspiration—and art can be a great source for that. This chapter is filled with lessons and games that use art—both ready-made and student-created—to help kids find their muses again. Use these activities to cure that outbreak of boredom infecting your writers.

Surprising Symmetry

In a Nutshell

There's nothing like a little paint splatter to get those creative juices flowing! In this activity, students use eyedroppers and poster paint to make symmetrical images. They will really stretch their **creative-thinking** muscles by imagining shapes in their artwork and practicing **expressive writing** as they describe what they see.

Teacher Bonus: The time and energy you invest in prepping for this messy lesson will be paid back in student enthusiasm for writing.

Plan Ahead

✍ Cover desks with newspaper.

✍ Set up a newspaper-covered area for drying artwork.

✍ Fill small plastic cups half full of poster paint mixed with a few drops of water to make it a runny consistency. Each cup will need an eyedropper. (The ones used in school science labs work great.) Straws also work, but students may need to be taught how to hold paint in them by covering one end with a thumb.

✍ Each student will need several sheets of inexpensive white paper (such as copy paper).

✍ Reproduce <u>1</u> class set of Surprising Symmetry Description worksheets (page 46). *Hint: Reproduce some extras so early finishers can complete more descriptions about different designs.*

How It Works

Take a deep breath and accept that this activity will be messy. Just make sure you prep the area so the mess won't be permanent. Students begin by folding a sheet of white paper in half. They will drop blobs of paint onto only one half of the paper. Then, they will fold the paper over the painted section and blot the ink onto the other half of the paper. Each finished design should be symmetrical.

As they create, ask students to tell their neighbors about the shapes they see in their designs. Circulate and make suggestions that push their thinking beyond the ordinary. Praise creative thinking!

When the artwork is dry, ask students to select one or two of their designs to write about. Hand out the Surprising Symmetry Description worksheets (page 46). The assignment is to write a description of the images in the designs. For this expressive writing assignment, students will focus on explaining their ideas clearly and include as much detail as possible.

After the mess is all cleaned up, display students' writing and artwork together on a bulletin board.

Differentiation Tip

Extend the lesson by asking students to make their symmetrical images the inspiration for a picture book.

Surprising Symmetry Description

Your Name: _____

Take a close look at the symmetrical pictures you made. Choose one design to write about. On the lines below, write a description of the image you see in the design. Your goal is to explain your ideas clearly and include as much detail as possible.

_____

_____

_____

_____

_____

_____

_____

_____

_____

_____

_____

Cut and Paste the Old-Fashioned Way

In a Nutshell

You knew you were saving those old magazines for a reason. Well, here it is! The hardest part of writing isn't the actual writing, it's *thinking* about what to write. When students get to cut and paste a story using words and phrases borrowed from magazines instead of having to think of them all on their own, pressure is relieved and minds are opened.

Teacher Bonus: This activity can be freeing for students with learning disabilities, especially those who have word-recall issues. At the same time, it challenges higher-level thinking by asking students to synthesize disparate ideas into a coherent story.

Plan Ahead

- ✍ Collect magazines, newspapers, brochures, and even old direct-mail pieces that can be cut apart.

- ✍ Each student will need scissors, markers, a glue stick, and a large piece of construction paper.

How It Works

Invite students to browse through print materials and cut out words and phrases that catch their attention. As piles of words grow, ask students to look for connections among ideas. Is there a common theme? Are several of the words related to the same topic (animals or music, for example)? Is a story idea forming? Circulate and assist students in making connections.

When students have a story idea in mind, the rest of their clippings should (perhaps loosely) build on the identified theme. Challenge students to gather 15 to 25 words and phrases. When they have done that, they can begin pasting their stories onto the large paper. Allow students to add in some basic words with markers as they compose.

The goal is to get students to synthesize ideas into a coherent narrative. You may need to remind students that the assignment is to compose a story. The stories may be strange and far-fetched, but they need to have a beginning, middle, and end. Simply gluing weird words into a list does not meet the assignment's parameters.

Make time for volunteers to share their wacky creations.

Differentiation Tip

For struggling students, reduce the number of words and phrases they are required to collect. Help them organize their collection of words into several stacks by topic.

"Be Mine, Hot Stuff," Said the Spoon to the Soup

In a Nutshell

Conversation hearts are a Valentine's Day tradition, but using them to write inanimate-object love stories is the last thing your students will expect. In fact, your students will be so flustered, they'll forget to complain about practicing their **dialogue-writing** skills!

Teacher Bonus: This activity can replace those old Valentine's Day crosswords and word searches. It's a holiday lesson with some real teaching power.

Plan Ahead

✍ Each student will need glue, markers, a large piece of construction paper, and a small box or bag of conversation hearts.

✍ Reproduce <u>1</u> overhead transparency of Sample Instrument Dialogue (page 43). *Hint: The rules for punctuating dialogue are many. Still, kids love to put dialogue in their stories, so it's a skill worth teaching and re-teaching. Just don't expect mastery on the first try!*

How It Works

Introduce this activity by telling your students that they get to write love stories in honor of the most romantic day of the year. You could even play this up by putting on a CD of romantic music and using your most mushy, gushy voice. Most likely, your students will begin to groan and gag. That's when you tell them not to worry. These will be silly love stories between inanimate, or non-living, objects, like a pencil and an eraser or a tube of toothpaste and a toothbrush. Then, begin handing out the bags of conversation hearts, and their feelings of dread will turn to excitement.

Students will first read each conversation heart in their stash. They will then use those words and phrases as inspiration for choosing two inanimate objects to be characters in a love dialogue. The words on the candy will be used in the conversations between the objects. (To ensure that students write a full story, require a specific number of candies to be used in the stories. Encourage students to trade hearts with classmates, if needed.)

Review the Sample Instrument Dialogue overhead transparency (page 43). Leave the overhead up as a resource for students to use during writing.

When students have chosen their characters and the candies they plan to use, they can begin writing with markers on the construction paper. As they write, they will glue the candy hearts where the words and phrases fit into the conversation. *(Hint: For this assignment, a rough draft really takes the fun out of using the candy hearts and turns a quick holiday activity into a multi-day project. Encourage students to plan their stories in their minds and work slowly to do their best the first time.)*

The finished products will make a colorful Valentine's Day bulletin board.

Differentiation Tip

To help students organize their ideas for writing, have them line up their candy hearts in the order they plan to use them in their stories.

Old Calendars, New Ideas

In a Nutshell

Help students warm up their brains with this fun, simple **creative-thinking** exercise. This workout uses art from old calendars to stretch those creative-thinking muscles.

Teacher Bonus: This is a one-time-prep activity.

Plan Ahead

✍ Collect a variety of art from old calendars.

✍ Laminate your favorite pictures to save in a Writing Ideas file that students can access anytime.

✍ Each student will need writing paper and a pencil.

How It Works

Begin by showing students a piece of calendar art. Ask two or three questions about it that will stretch your students' creative-thinking muscles. Have students write responses in a writer's notebook to save for later use in stories and poetry. Allow time for sharing after each picture, because that should help those who are struggling for ideas. In this activity, the focus is on the thinking process rather than on the final product. Treat it as a warm up; and don't get hung up on spelling, grammar, and punctuation. With practice, the creative questioning will come easily. Here are some suggestions to get you started:

Questions for animal photos (*a student favorite!*)

* *What is this animal thinking?*
* *What are these animals saying to each other?*

Questions for photos/paintings of people *(Try Picasso's cubist portraits!)*

* *What is this person's name?*
* *What is this person's occupation?*
* *Describe this person's family.*
* *What is this person's favorite food? color? song? movie? vacation spot?*
* *Why does this person look sad (happy, distracted, cranky, etc.)?*

Questions for landscape photos/paintings

* *What kinds of people or animals live here?*
* *What mystery might have happened here?*
* *If you took a trip to this place, what would you pack in your suitcase?*

Questions for abstract art

* *What do you see in this picture?*
* *What was the artist thinking about when creating this artwork?*
* *If this painting/photo could talk, what would it say?*

Differentiation Tip

If you anticipate that some students will struggle to keep up, create a list of questions for them to answer on paper. Having the questions in print might be helpful for some.

Turn Words into Works of Art

In a Nutshell

Cement students love of poetry by assigning **concrete poems**. Without all of the rules about syllables and rhyme patterns, these poems are a hit with students. They get to choose a subject, write a few descriptive sentences about it, and then shape their words into works of art.

Teacher Bonus: This activity requires little advance preparation. That makes it perfect for those days when unexpected events derail your regularly scheduled lesson.

Plan Ahead

✍ Reproduce <u>1</u> class set of Concrete Poetry Examples worksheets (page 51) and Concrete Poetry Practice worksheets (page 52).

✍ Each student will need several sheets of unlined white paper and a pencil. Markers and construction paper are optional.

✍ *Optional:* Share examples of concrete poetry with your class. Two great examples are *Doodle Dandies: Poems That Take Shape* by J. Patrick Lewis and *A Poke in the I: A Collection of Concrete Poems* compiled by Paul B. Janeczko.

How It Works

Concrete poems take the shape of the poem's subject. For example, a poem about a rainbow might be written in arching lines that mimic a rainbow's shape; a poem about a baseball game might be written in the shape of a baseball diamond. Other than the shape rule, there are no parameters to follow—which is why kids love this type of poetry. It doesn't have to rhyme!

If possible, begin this lesson by showing your students several examples of concrete poems (page 51). Then, ask students to choose a subject to describe in a concrete poem. Remind them that the best writing comes from what they know well and have experienced, so their subject should be something familiar to them. If they've never seen a manatee, then a manatee is a poor topic choice for them. If they love soccer, dogs, and ice-cream sundaes, those would be excellent subject choices.

Hand out the Concrete Poetry Practice worksheets (page 52). These worksheets are for students to organize their thoughts and write a rough draft before working on the poem's shape. Preview the assignment together and remind students that all poetry uses vivid verbs, similes, metaphors, and juicy details to paint crystal clear pictures with words. When they (and you) are satisfied with their descriptions, it's time to get artistic! Students can form their paragraphs into pictures on white paper or construction paper. This may take several tries to get the words to fit the way they want them to. If time allows, encourage students to do a final draft in colored pencil or marker. Finally, mount the finished products on colorful construction paper and display them in a prominent place in the classroom or school building.

Differentiation Tip

Challenge students by requiring them to include at least one simile and one metaphor in their poems.

Concrete Poetry Examples

A Summer Treat

Ice cream is my
favorite summer treat.
Mint chocolate chip, bubblegum,
strawberry, rainbow sherbet, cookie
dough, chocolate peanut butter.
Cool and refreshing,
creamy and sweet—
What a great
way to
beat
the
heat!

Little Mouse

Little mouse,
you are so tiny and cute.
Your bubblegum pink nose sniffs the air.
Your two front teeth chomp on invisible cheese.
You scurry through our kitchen on your little feet, just as cute as you can be.
"Look, Mom, it's a cute little mouse," I said.
I don't understand it, but she jumped
on a chair and started
screaming.

Concrete Poetry Practice

Your Name: _____

Concrete poems are poems written in the shape of the subjects they describe. But before you can form the words into the shape, you need to know what you are going to write!

Get a Topic!

Writers do their best writing when they write about what they know. Make a list of at least five topics you know a lot about.

_____

Get Descriptive!

Choose one topic from the list above. Write a short paragraph (about five sentences) describing it. Use five-senses details, vivid verbs, metaphors, and similes to paint a picture with your words.

_____

_____

_____

_____

_____

Get Concrete!

Now it's time to get artistic. Use white paper and a pencil to begin forming your words into a shape. Remember, the shape should come from the topic of your poem. When it looks the way you want it to, use coloring supplies to complete a final draft.

WANTED: Creative Thinking

In a Nutshell

In this easy-to-prepare activity, students get to stretch their creativity into the criminal realm by creating humorous WANTED posters. Along with exercising **creative thinking**, this activity also challenges students to write with juicy **details**.

Teacher Bonus: This activity is a one-time-prep activity. Collect the pictures and store them in a Writing Ideas file that you and your students can access anytime.

Plan Ahead

✍ Cut out pictures of men, women, cartoons, and even strange objects from magazines and catalogs. Choose subjects that range from ordinary to outlandish. Glue each picture onto a different piece of construction paper and laminate for longevity.

✍ Reproduce <u>1</u> class set of Wanted Poster worksheets (page 54). *Hint: Reproduce some extras so early finishers can complete more posters about different criminals.*

How It Works

Distribute the laminated pictures, and tell students they are photos of criminals. It can be fun to make up a story to go along with the activity. For example, announce to the class, "The local police department needs your help finding these criminals. It won't be easy, but with your writing skills, the police hope to capture all of them by the end of the week."

Assign students the task of creating posters to go with the criminal photos they have in front of them. Explain that WANTED posters are tools used by the police and the F.B.I. to get ordinary citizens to help find criminals. They must be written so clearly and in such great detail that people could recognize the criminal from the written descriptions. Now, hand out the worksheets (page 54) to students. Preview the assignment together. You may need to explain the term "aliases."

Remind students which topics are school-appropriate and which are off limits. Be up front by saying that anybody could make up a murderer, but you're looking for creative thinkers who go beyond the obvious. Get them on the right track by modeling appropriate topics. For example, a heavily-made-up woman might be wanted for robbing mall makeup counters, or a male model might be so vain that he's wanted for stealing mirrors from department store dressing rooms. Higher-level thinkers can understand the basic principle of humor writing—it's funny because it's true. Push them to find the humor inherent in the picture they were given. Encourage them to find a main idea—some key piece of information about the criminal—on which to base their details.

Differentiation Tip

Ask students to write an A.P.B. (all-points bulletin), a public broadcast asking citizens to help locate suspects on the loose. The writing must be clear and detailed so that people could recognize the suspect from the description. Display all the criminal photos and read the A.P.B.'s aloud. Ask the class to try to match the photos to the descriptions. This acts as an assessment of the lesson's effectiveness.

Wanted Poster

Your Name: _____

WANTED

Criminal Name: _____

Aliases: _____

_____

Height: _____

Weight: _____

Eye Color: _____

Hair (color and description): _____

_____

Distinguishing Features: _____

_____

Often Seen: _____

_____

_____

Unusual Traits and Habits:

_____

_____

_____

_____

Student Superheroes to the Rescue!

In a Nutshell

The superhero is an irresistible figure in our culture. In this lesson, students will explore their own superpowers and get those writing ideas flowing faster than a speeding bullet! Okay, so they won't be able to leap tall buildings in a single bound, but they will be able to write a great **narrative story** in the form of a **comic strip**.

Teacher Bonus: This is a great activity to inspire students who struggle with writing. Writing a comic strip is still great practice with narrative writing, but it is less daunting than writing a whole short story.

Plan Ahead

✐ Reproduce <u>1</u> class set of You Are the Superhero! worksheets (page 56) and <u>1</u> class set of Star in Your Own Comic Strip! worksheets (page 57).

✐ Students will need a pencil and coloring supplies (colored pencils would work best).

✐ *Optional:* Share examples of superheroes with your students. Superman, Batman, Spiderman, and Wonder Woman would be the traditional examples. For more ethnically diverse examples, check out the Green Lantern from the Justice League, Storm from The X-Men, Tarantula from Nightwing, Apache Chief from the Superfriends, and Mercy Man. The novel series *Shredderman* by Wendelin Van Draanen would also be a great model for this activity.

How It Works

Share some superhero examples with your class. Explain that superheroes often first came from the imaginations of people who were bullied in real life. It was their way of using their talents (drawing, writing, and creativity) rather than fists to right the wrongs they had experienced.

Ask students to begin thinking about the type of wrongs they would like to right in their worlds. What really bugs them? What would they like to change about the world if only they had the superpowers to do it? It could be small things, like too much homework, or it could be big things, like helping the homeless. Make a list of their ideas.

Hand out the You Are the Superhero! worksheets (page 56). Read the directions together and preview the assignment. If you think it would help, model the activity on an overhead transparency. Create your own SuperTeacher superhero who rights the wrongs of the classroom, like stopping cheaters and finding missing homework. Have fun with the possibilities and tailor it to the issues in your classroom.

When students have had a chance to create their superheroes, hand out the Star in Your Own Comic Strip worksheets (page 57). Ask students to write and illustrate a comic strip in which their superhero is a main character. Just like all narrative writing, the comic strip needs all the elements of a story—characters, plot, setting, theme, and mood. Its plot must have a clear beginning, middle, and end.

Differentiation Tip

Challenge students to create a comic book in which their superheroes star in a longer narrative story.

You Are the Superhero!

Your Name: _____

On the outline below, add facial features, a costume, and tools to create your own superhero identity. Remember, the clothing and tools should reflect the superhero's superpowers and mission.

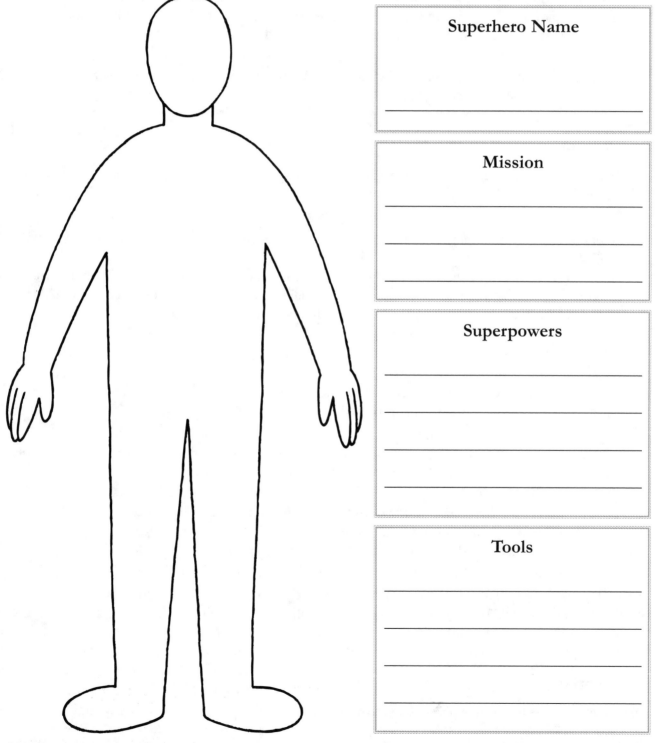

Superhero Name

_____

Mission

_____

_____

_____

Superpowers

_____

_____

_____

_____

Tools

_____

_____

_____

_____

Star in Your Own Comic Strip!

Your Name: _____

Now it's time for your superhero to save the day! The superhero you created will be the main character in a comic strip. The comic strip must have a clear beginning, middle, and end. And don't forget the action!

What's My Line?

In a Nutshell

Have you ever seen a toddler more fascinated by the box a toy came in than with the toy itself? Well, this simple writing game is the adolescent equivalent of that box. It's so simple, yet it provides hours of entertainment—and a bit of **creative writing** practice, too!

Teacher Bonus: This game requires no preparation. Pull out the idea when your class gets derailed without warning!

Plan Ahead

✍ You will need a writing utensil and something large to write on, like a dry-erase marker and a dry-erase board or a crayon and chart paper.

✍ Students will need a pencil and a writer's notebook or writing paper.

How It Works

Begin the game by drawing a simple line on the board or on chart paper. It does not have to be a straight line—and in fact, squiggly or jagged lines are better. Hand the marker to a student and ask him or her to add onto the line. Have that student hand the marker to a classmate who will add onto the line again. Continue passing the pen until an interesting shape appears.

Now, ask students to look carefully at the shape. What picture or pictures do they see? Ask them to describe what they see in a short paragraph or to write a short story about the picture.

Allow time for students to read their writing aloud. That will help inspire students who are struggling with the exercise. Begin a new round of the game with another simple line and continue play as time allows.

Differentiation Tip

Make the game more challenging by asking students to write a poem instead of a description. Make it even more challenging by requiring a specific type of poem, such as a haiku or a limerick.

Storyboard an Action Sequence

In a Nutshell

It's no surprise that kids growing up in the age of video games get a thrill from action stories. It follows, then, that they would want to include action in their own stories. But **action sequences** aren't easy to write. Too often, kids skim over the "good stuff" in their writing because the good stuff is complicated. Try this storyboarding activity to get your students to envision the action before they try to write about it.

Teacher Bonus: This activity packs a powerful punch for many reluctant writers. When you start talking action, they start listening!

Plan Ahead

✍ Reproduce <u>1</u> overhead transparency of the Action! Story Starter (page 60).

✍ Students will need a pencil and large, white drawing paper divided into six boxes or frames. Students can do the dividing themselves by folding the paper in half lengthwise and then folding it in thirds the opposite way.

✍ *Optional:* Share examples of movie storyboards with students. George Lucas, the creator of the *Star Wars* movies, is famous for using storyboards to plan out his films. Some examples are available online and in books, such as *Star Wars Episode I: The Phantom Menace, The Illustrated Screenplay* by George Lucas, and *Revenge of the Sith Movie Storybook* by Alice Alfonsi.

How It Works

Explain that storyboards are a way for movie directors to get a glimpse of action sequences before yelling "Action!" Many directors hire artists to illustrate each action sequence frame by frame. The finished storyboards look like comic strips of the movies.

Display the overhead transparency of the Action! Story Starter (page 60). Read it aloud to students. Leave it on display for them to reread as necessary. The story stops before it gets to the "good stuff." Ask students to begin to think about an action-packed ending to the story. What will happen step by step? How exactly will Adam escape?

Hand out the white drawing paper to students. Ask them to focus on the "good stuff" that was left out of the story. They will draw the imagined action sequences out step by step in storyboard form. The emphasis here here should be on ideas rather than artistic ability. Encourage students to use stick figures, if necessary—as long as they are sketching the action step by step.

When their storyboards are completed, students will write two or three sentences describing each frame. Allow time for students to read their endings aloud. Wrap up the lesson by discussing how planning can make an action sequence much easier to write and much more thrilling to read.

Differentiation Tip

To simplify the activity, allow students to illustrate and write about three frames of action instead of six.

Action! Story Starter

The Beast in the Alley

It was almost 9:00 p.m., and I still had one last chore left to do before my mom would give me my allowance for the week. I had to take out the garbage. Okay, I know you're probably thinking, "What's the big deal? Just take out the trash already!"

Well, normally I would have no problem. But tonight I was in no hurry to drag those trashcans to the end of the alley behind our house. You see, I had overheard some older kids on my bus talking about a beast lurking in the alley. I knew they were probably just trying to freak out us younger kids, but I have to admit, it worked. And now I'd put off taking out the trash for so long that it was dark outside. It's not that I was afraid, exactly, but I just didn't want to come face to face with any beast, if you know what I mean.

"Adam, take out the trash right this minute!" my mom yelled at me.

I knew I couldn't put it off any longer. I took a deep breath and dragged the two trashcans out of the garage and into the alley. I looked both ways and didn't see anything spooky, so I started walking toward the street.

When I was halfway down the alley, that's when I heard it—a deep growl that sounded like a cross between a wolf and a bear. I froze. The growl got louder and turned into a hiss. I knew I had to get back to my garage, but how?

You take it from here! How will Adam get out of the alley and away from the beast? Draw out the action sequence frame by frame, like a storyboard for an action movie. When you're finished drawing, write two or three sentences about each picture to describe the action so readers will feel like they're seeing a movie!

Get Out!

THE GREAT OUTDOORS INSPIRES GREAT WRITING.

You know the symptoms—slumped shoulders, deep frowns, and glassy eyes fixed on the scene outside the classroom windows. It's obvious that your students have caught spring fever or first-snowfall fever or sunny-day-after-lots-of-rain fever. Your students' minds have wandered right out into the elements, and they're not coming back for a five-paragraph essay prompt. But don't close those blinds, and don't even think about giving up your writing time! When students are fascinated by the world outside the windows, send them out into it. This chapter is filled with lessons and games that use the great outdoors as inspiration for great writing.

Cloud Conversations

In a Nutshell

When was the last time you looked up at the clouds and saw a dragon or a mermaid? In our hectic world, most of us—even kids—don't have time to see shapes in the clouds these days. So, make the time, and it just might make your students more creative writers.

Teacher Bonus: All you really need for this activity is a sky filled with fluffy clouds.

Plan Ahead

✍ Check the sky to make sure there are clouds in it.

✍ Reproduce 1 class set of One Cloud Said to Another worksheets (page 63) as a time-saving template for the dialogue. *Hint: Reproduce some extras so early finishers can complete more conversations.*

✍ Students will need a writer's notebook; a pencil; and for step 2, a One Cloud Said to Another worksheet (page 63). *Hint: If students are using lined paper, make sure they take a clipboard, a notebook, or some other hard surface to use as a lapboard.*

✍ *Optional:* When the weather starts to get nice, ask students to bring in beach towels to keep in their lockers for outside writing activities like this one.

How It Works

Wait for a beautiful spring day when the sky is filled with puffy clouds. Lead your students out to the playground or the ball field with their writer's notebooks. Spread out on the ground, look up, and study the cloud shapes. Explain to students that they should look for shapes in the clouds. If students seem confused, take the lead and model some examples aloud: "That one looks like a spaceship with an alien peeking out the window." "That one looks like a flying puppy." Pretty soon, everyone will be sharing ideas. Remember, the goal is to spark creativity. It's okay if some students seem to be coming up with outlandish ideas that don't match any of the clouds in the sky. Students should make a list of their cloud-shape sightings in their writer's notebooks.

For the second step of the activity, ask students to choose two of the shapes or creatures on their list and write a dialogue between them. Hand out the One Cloud Said to Another worksheet (page 63). You might need to jump start the process by modeling a dialogue of your own. If you want to use this activity to reinforce dialogue punctuation rules, you could also use the Sample Instrument Dialogue reproducible (page 43).

Differentiation Tip

Extend the activity by challenging students to write a fantasy story with the cloud shapes as main characters.

One Cloud Said to Another

Your Name: _____

Character 1 _____ : " _____

_____ "

Character 2 _____ : " _____

_____ "

_____ : " _____

_____ "

_____ : " _____

_____ "

_____ : " _____

_____ "

_____ : " _____

_____ "

_____ : " _____

_____ "

See Nature from a New Perspective

In a Nutshell

Looking at the world from a different **point of view** is challenging for young people, but it's an exercise that can make them better writers and better people. Students will write their own day-in-the-life journals from the perspective of an object found in nature. This is also an exercise in **personification**.

Plan Ahead

✍ *Optional:* Borrow or buy *Diary of a Worm* and/or *Diary of a Spider* by Doreen Cronin.

✍ For Step 2, reproduce <u>1</u> class set of Think Like a Rock worksheets (page 65).

✍ For Step 2, students will need a pencil and a Think Like a Rock worksheet (page 65). *Hint: Make sure students have a hard surface to use as a lapboard outdoors.*

✍ For Step 3, students will need pencils and enough sheets of paper to complete the number of diary entries you assigned.

How It Works

Step 1—Get Inspired. You could begin this activity by reading *Diary of a Worm* or *Diary of a Spider* by Doreen Cronin to your class. Call attention to the details that really illuminate the critters' viewpoints and make the stories funny. For example, in *Diary of a Worm*, the main character is terrified of kids playing hopscotch, his playmate is a spider, and his father eats the newspaper instead of reading it. These are the details that twist reality to make the story funny. If you don't have the books to use as models, don't worry. Skip Step 1 and start with Step 2.

Step 2—Think Like a Rock. Next, take your class outside to observe nature on the playground or on the ball field. Ask students to choose a creature or an object—a dandelion, a rock, a blade of grass, a wood chip, a leaf, an insect, etc. Hand out the Think Like a Rock worksheets (page 65). The worksheet is designed to get students to think like their natural object. Ask students to work on creatively answering the questions. You might model two or three answers to get students started on the right track. For example, a dandelion might love the color yellow, hate windy days, and fear lawnmowers. Her friends are the blades of grass all around her and her most embarrassing moment is when the wind blows away her fluffy white "skirt" and leaves her standing in the yard naked.

Step 3—Write Like a Rock. Finally, students will write several (assign based on time and ability) day-in-the-life diary entries from the perspectives of their natural objects. Have them do this on lined paper or in their Writer's Notebooks. Remind them that the humor will come from those essential truths that they observed in nature.

Differentiation Tip

Extend the activity by challenging students to write and illustrate a picture book with their natural object as the main character.

Think Like a Rock

(Or Other Natural Object)

Your Name: _____

My natural object is a _____

I imagine that my natural object is a (*circle one*)   **boy**   **girl**

After studying my natural object, I imagine that its personality
would be

_____

My natural object . . .

    likes   _____

    dislikes   _____

    fears   _____

My natural object would be embarrassed if _____

My natural object would be happy if _____

My natural object would be sad if _____

My natural object would be proud if _____

My natural object is friends with _____

My natural object is enemies with _____

My natural object's hobbies are _____

_____

My natural object's dream or goal in life is _____

_____

Take a Simile and Metaphor Hike

In a Nutshell

What better place to find inspiration for **descriptive writing** than the great outdoors? When practicing **similes** and **metaphors**, take your class on a hike to observe the many colors, shapes, and textures of nature. Later, they can turn their observations into simile and metaphor poems.

Plan Ahead

✍ For Step 1, reproduce <u>1</u> class set of Searching for Similes and Metaphors worksheets (page 67).

✍ For Step 1, students will need a pencil and a Searching for Similes and Metaphors worksheet (page 67). *Hint: Make sure students have a hard surface to use as a lapboard outdoors.*

✍ For Step 2, reproduce <u>1</u> class set of Nature Poetry worksheets (page 68).

How It Works

Step 1—Take a Hike. Take your class on a hike around the school grounds. Have each student bring a pencil, a Searching for Similes and Metaphors worksheet (page 67), and a hard surface to use as a lapboard. Review the definitions of similes and metaphors. A *simile* is a comparison that uses "like" or "as" (for example, "The pond is as smooth as glass," "The sky is blue like the ocean," "The frog leapt as gracefully as a ballerina."). A *metaphor* is a stronger, more direct comparison that omits the "like" or "as" (for example, "The clouds are cotton balls," "The leafless oak tree is a skeleton."). Have students examine the world around them and complete the Searching for Similes and Metaphors worksheet by writing original similes and metaphors for the things they see.

Step 2—Get Descriptive. Students will now use their observations to write a five-line nature poem describing an object they observed. Hand out the Nature Poetry worksheets (page 68). The poems do not have to rhyme!

Differentiation Tip

Notice how the sample poem uses related imagery to describe the grass as nature's army. The similes and metaphors work together to build on a single theme. If some students are ready for this challenge, push them to tie each simile and metaphor together in theme and in tone. The finished product will be a much stronger poem.

Searching for Similes and Metaphors

Your Name: _____

| Look for similes in nature. A **simile** is a comparison that uses "like" or "as." Write your similes on the lines below. | Look for metaphors in nature. A **metaphor** is a stronger, more direct comparison that does not use "like" or "as." Write your metaphors on the lines below. |

The pond is as smooth as glass.

The frog leapt like an NBA player dunking a ball.

The clouds are cotton ball.

The leafless oak tree is a skeleton.

Nature Poetry

Your Name: _____

Now it's time to turn your similes and metaphors into poetry. Choose an object you saw in nature.
Read the sample poem below for inspiration. Then, fill in the blanks below. You'll soon be writing
poems like a natural!

> Nature's Army
> Blades of grass
> As straight as swords
> As sharp as arrows
> Green like army uniforms
> Soldiers on a battlefield

_____

Title

_____

Name of Object(s)

_____

Simile using "as"

_____

Simile using "as"

_____

Simile using "like"

_____

Metaphor

Skip, Strut, Skid!
Show Off Those Vivid Verbs!

In a Nutshell

Actions speak louder than words—especially to a room full of fidgety kids. Instead of just telling students to replace boring verbs with vivid verbs, show them how. Actually, have *them* show *you* the difference a vivid verb can make.

Plan Ahead

✍ Reproduce <u>1</u> class set of Vivid Verbs worksheets (page 70).

✍ Students will need a pencil and a Vivid Verbs worksheet (page 70). *Hint: Make sure students have a hard surface to use as a lapboard outdoors.*

How It Works

Take your class out to the playground or ball field. Have students sit so everyone can see the action. Hand out the Vivid Verbs worksheets (page 70). Invite a volunteer to walk back and forth in front of the class. As he or she walks, have students call out vivid verbs to replace the dull word "walk." A few examples have been provided on the worksheet to get the action started. The volunteer should change his or her gait to fit the words being called. Be prepared to demonstrate some of the more unique suggestions that the volunteer may not know how to act out. Also, keep students on track by making sure their verbs are correct synonyms for the word they replace. The goal is to make their verb usage more accurate in writing, not more bizarre. For example, "run" does not replace "walk" accurately and would not belong on the replacement list. During the demonstration, students should keep a list of the vivid verbs they hear. Repeat the activity for the other boring verbs on the worksheet.

Ask students to keep their completed Vivid Verbs worksheets in a safe place to use as a reference for writing. When editing future assignments, encourage students to change their dull verbs into vivid ones.

Differentiation Tip

Extend the activity by challenging students to come up with other boring verbs and their vivid replacements. Or, turn the activity into a game by awarding prizes to the students who come up with the longest list of vivid verbs to replace the word "walk."

Get Out!

Skip, Strut, Skid! Show Off Those Vivid Verbs!

Vivid Verbs

Your Name: _____

Vivid verbs are specific action words that paint pictures in readers' minds. Unlike boring verbs, vivid verbs spice up writing and make action more exciting. In the chart below, make a list of vivid verbs that could replace the boring verb at the top of each column. When you're finished, save this chart to help you replace dull verbs in your own writing.

Walk	**Say/Said**	**Run**
strut saunter	yell groan	zoom
trudge stomp		
Dance	**Look**	**Ask**
boogie	stare	beg

See the Writing on the Walls . . . and Walkways

In a Nutshell

Sometimes it's not what you write, but what you write *with* that matters to kids. All you need for this activity is a box of sidewalk chalk and an expanse of dry pavement or a brick wall. Take your class outside and let them spill their creativity all over the sidewalk with this simple, shared-writing relay. It's the perfect cure for spring fever!

Teacher Bonus: This game requires little advance preparation, making it perfect for when unexpected events—or a beautiful day—derail your regularly scheduled lesson.

Plan Ahead

✐ You will need <u>1</u> box of sidewalk chalk.

✐ Get an official "O.K." for students to write with chalk on the school's outdoor walls, walkways, or playground. If your administrators won't want to wait for the rain to clean up the mess, promise to clean up after the game is over. In that case, you'll need to add buckets and sponges to your list of materials for this activity.

How It Works

On one of those perfect, cloudless days, take your students outside for writing. Divide the class into four or five heterogeneous writing teams, and have each team form a single-file line. Make sure each team has enough surface area (on a wall, a sidewalk, or a playground) to write a few paragraphs in chalk. Hand out a piece of chalk to the first person in each team's line.

This game is a writing relay. You will call out a letter of the alphabet. The first person in line must write a sentence beginning with that letter. When that person has finished, he or she will hand off the chalk to the next person in line. The next person will write a second sentence beginning with the next letter in the alphabet. For example, if the first sentence had to start with "D," the second sentence will start with "E," the third with "F," and so on until each person on the team has written a sentence. (*Hint: The first time you play the game, start with the letter "A."*) Each sentence should build on the first sentence to create a story that makes at least a little bit of sense. Here is an example:

A cat ran across the street.

Boys on bikes slammed on their brakes.

"**C**razy cat!" shouted one boy.

"**D**on't do that anymore," said another.

"**E**eeek!" hissed the cat.

From that day on, the cat made sure to look both ways before crossing the street.

The first team to finish the relay wins that round and gets to read their wacky story aloud to the class after all teams have completed the race. Continue playing as time allows.

Differentiation Tip

Make the game more challenging by starting with a less common letter, like "Q." Make it even more challenging by designating a subject that all stories have to be about, such as sports, animals, or fast food.

Sing Campfire Songs Around the Jungle Gym

In a Nutshell

You don't need a campfire to inspire students to write their own campfire songs. Kids love to make up silly **rhymes**, so encourage them to get creative. Then, plan a day when the class can share their wacky lyrics around an imaginary campfire.

Teacher Bonus: This activity fits perfectly into a poetry unit and will quickly change the attitudes of students who assume poetry is sappy and dull.

Plan Ahead

✎ Reproduce 1 Around the Campfire worksheet (page 73) for every pair of students.

✎ *Optional*: On the campfire-song-sharing day, bring a snack of trail mix or s'mores for students to enjoy as they celebrate their hard work.

How It Works

Ask students if they know any campfire songs or chants. If they are willing to sing them for the class, remind them that the lyrics must be school-appropriate. If students can't think of examples, two well-known campfire songs are "Going on a Bear Hunt" and "Down by the Banks." If you would like more examples, an Internet search for campfire songs could be helpful. Here are the lyrics to "Down by the Banks":

Down by the Banks

Down by the banks of the Hanky Panky,
Where the bullfrogs jump from bank to bank-y
With a hip-hop, flippity-flop,
Missed the bank-y and went ker-plop.

Point out that these songs have several things in common: they are usually about nature, they rhyme, and the words are simple and often nonsensical. Make sure students understand the campfire-song genre before proceeding with the lesson.

Next, match each student with a partner. Hand out the Around the Campfire worksheets (page 73) to each pair of students. Partners will work together to write an original, rhyming campfire chant.

When students have had time to write and practice their campfire songs, give them a chance to share them with their classmates. Plan a campfire sing-along for students to gather outdoors in a circle and teach each other their rhymes. You could make the event more fun by making a fake campfire out of empty paper towel rolls and colored tissue paper. Bringing in traditional campfire snacks, like trail mix or s'mores, would also make the activity memorable for students.

Differentiation Tip

For those who are struggling, make rhyming explicit by modeling the process. Take the word you want to rhyme and remove the first letter. Then, go through the alphabet and try each letter at the beginning of the word to see what words you can make.

Around the Campfire

Your Name: _____

Singing songs around the campfire is a tradition. Now it's your turn to write a campfire song that your classmates will love to sing. Start by picking a topic from nature, like an animal, a landform, or an outdoor activity. Then, come up with at least four or five statements about that topic and make sure they rhyme. Practice singing your campfire song to make sure it's catchy and easy to sing. See the sample below.

Down by the Banks

Down by the banks of the Hanky Panky,
Where the bullfrogs jump from bank to bank-y
With a hip-hop, flippity-flop,
Missed the bank-y and went ker-plop.

Topic Ideas: _____ _____ _____ _____

Circle the one topic you and your partner have chosen to write your campfire song about.

_____

_____

_____

_____

_____

_____

_____

_____

Plan a Mountain Man's Menu

In a Nutshell

Imagine a meal of fried slugs dipped in mud sauce. How about a sweet grass salad drizzled with acorn vinaigrette? Or would you rather start with the dandelion stew? Writing original recipes using only ingredients found on the school grounds may not make mouths water, but it will spice up **expository writing** practice.

Teacher Bonus: This lesson could tie in to social studies units about Native Americans, explorers, early colonization, the Revolutionary War (soldiers got very hungry at Valley Forge!), and westward expansion.

Plan Ahead

✍ Reproduce <u>1</u> Recipe Card worksheet (page 75) for each student. *Hint: Reproduce some extras so early finishers can write more recipes.*

✍ Students will need a pencil, a piece of lined paper (or their Writer's Notebooks), and a Recipe Card worksheet (page 75). *Hint: Make sure students have a hard surface to use as a lapboard outdoors.*

✍ *Optional:* Bring cookbooks and recipe cards for examples.

How It Works

Many chefs use local ingredients in their gourmet dishes. In keeping with that trend, take your students outside to find inspiration for original recipes using ingredients found locally—in other words, on the school grounds. Before you turn your students loose to write, you may allow them to browse through cookbooks to get familiar with how recipes are written.

Have students search the school grounds and make a list of possible ingredients in their Writer's Notebooks or on lined paper. Most of them will really love to imagine cooking with the disgusting things they find.

When students have a list of 10–20 possible ingredients to work with, hand out the Recipe Card Worksheets (page 75). Each student will create an original recipe, complete with title, ingredient list, and directions. Be sure to point out the specialized vocabulary found in cookbooks and encourage students to spice up their writing with fancy words and phrases, such as *garnish, a splash, sauté, marinade, a pinch*, and others. Writing a phrase like, "Add a splash of rain water to the clover marinade" will be funnier than writing "Mix in some rain water." "Sautee the ants until they caramelize" is more fun to write than "Cook ants." If time allows, students can plan an entire menu made with all-natural, all-local ingredients.

Differentiation Tip

Extend the activity by challenging students to write and illustrate entire cookbooks with separate sections for appetizers, soups and salads, sides, main dishes, desserts, and drinks.

Recipe Card

Name of Recipe: _____

From the natural kitchen of _____

Ingredients

_____

_____

_____

_____

Directions

Step 1: _____

_____

Step 2: _____

_____

Step 3: _____

_____

Step 4: _____

_____

Step 5: _____

_____

Informal Writing Assessments

Teacher Feedback Form 1

Name:	Assignment:

I liked . . .

Keep working on . . .

I have a question about . . .

- -

Teacher Feedback Form 2

Name:	Assignment:			
Focus on . . .	You mastered the technique! You showed that you understand how to use it to improve your writing.	You understand the technique. Keep working on using it to improve your writing.	Did you understand the technique? Let's work on using it to improve your writing.	Your work showed no evidence of the technique being used. Let's talk so that I can help you understand it.

Student Self-Assessment Checklist

Name: _____   **Assignment:** _____

Congratulations on finishing your assignment! Now it's time to think about the work you have done.
Read each sentence below. Think about your performance on this assignment. Put a checkmark
(✓) in the box that describes how you feel about your work.

	Yes	**No**	**Somewhat**
I worked hard on this assignment. I know I am turning in my best work.			
I understand the writing technique we are focusing on in class.			
I used the writing technique(s) we are focusing on in class to improve my work.			
I need more help understanding the writing technique we are focusing on in class.			
I proofread my work for spelling, grammar, capitalization, and punctuation errors.			
I followed all assignment directions carefully.			
I used my writing time wisely.			

Focus on Five Rubric

Name _____	Expectations	Points Earned (50 points possible)
Writing Craft	**Applied the writing technique of . . .**	
	(15 points possible)	
	Applied the writing technique of . . .	
	(15 points possible)	
Grammar	**Demonstrated mastery of . . .**	
	(10 points possible)	
	Correctly used . . .	
	(5 points possible)	
Conventions	**Correctly used . . .**	
	(5 points possible)	
	Comments:	**Total Points:**

Weighted Creative-Writing Rubric

Name _____	10	8.5	7	6–0
Writing Craft 60%	You mastered the technique! You showed that you understand how to use it to improve your writing.	You understand the technique. Keep working on using it to improve your writing.	Did you understand the technique? Let's work on using it to improve your writing.	Your work showed no evidence of the technique being used. Let's talk so that I can help you understand it.
Creativity 30%	Your writing is one-of-a-kind! It was fun to read!	Your writing showed originality. Next time, push that creativity even further!	Your writing had some unique elements. Next time, think about how you could make it more original.	Your writing did not show enough originality.
Conventions 10%	Your spelling, punctuation, capitalization and grammar were perfect!	It was hard to find spelling, punctuation, capitalization, or grammar errors in your work.	There were several spelling, punctuation, capitalization, or grammar errors in your work.	The number of spelling, punctuation, capitalization, and grammar errors in your work is unacceptable.
Score:				

- -

Weighted Creative-Writing Rubric Template

Name _____	10	8.5	7	6–0
Writing Craft _____%				
Creativity _____%				
Conventions _____%				
Score:				

How To Use the Weighted Creative-Writing Rubric

If you've never used a weighted rubric (see page 79), it can seem a little confusing at first glance. Once you understand how it works, though, you'll see that it gives you more control over the scoring process.

Reading the Rubric

The titles in the left column identify the skills or elements being graded. In this example, the teacher is grading for writing craft, overall creativity, and conventions. The percentages identify the weight assigned to each skill or element. As you can see, writing craft counts for more than half the total score (60%), creativity counts for 30%, and conventions counts for only 10% of the total score. These percentages must add up to 100%.

The numbers across the top roughly correspond to the letter grades A, B, C, and D/F. These numbers provide a rating for how the student performed in each of the areas assessed. Below each number is a description of what that score means for each element being graded. The descriptors make the grading standard clear to students and parents.

To use the rubric, circle one descriptor in each row to describe how the student performed in that skill or element. To compute the total score, multiply the whole number score assigned to each skill by the first number of the percentage for that skill. Then, add the three products to get a total percentage out of 100%. The sample rubric below has been done for you.

Step 1: Multiply

Writing Craft (60%): 10 x 6 = 60
Creativity (30%): 7 x 3 = 21
Conventions (10%): 8.5 x 1 = 8.5

Step 2: Add

60 + 21 + 8.5 = 89.5%

Name: *Kevin K.*	**10**	**8.5**	**7**	**6–0**
Writing Craft **60%** *Writing a Lead*	You mastered the technique! You showed that you understand how to use it to improve your writing.	You understand the technique. Keep working on using it to improve your writing.	Did you understand the technique? Let's work on using it to improve your writing.	Your work showed no evidence of the technique being used. Let's talk so that I can help you understand it.
Creativity **30 %**	Your writing is one-of-a-kind! It was fun to read!	Your writing showed originality. Next time, push that creativity even further!	Your writing had some unique elements. Next time, think about how you could make it more original.	Your writing showed no originality.
Conventions **10 %**	Your spelling, punctuation, capitalization and grammar were perfect!	It was hard to find spelling, punctuation, capitalization, or grammar errors in your work.	There were several spelling, punctuation, capitalization, or grammar errors in your work.	The number of spelling, punctuation, capitalization, and grammar errors in your work is unacceptable.
Score: *89.5%*				